Confessions

OF CHILD LOSS

Emily Graham

Cover Design by Finicky Fox Design
Author Image by Tara Kelly Photography
Published by Nine30 Publishing
Website: AfterChildLoss.com

ISBN 979-8-9865627-0-4

Dedication

To my favorite boy, Cameron. I always knew I would write something, someday. I never in a million years thought it would be this. It's not what I want, and you know I would give anything to rewrite the ending, but we can't. You changed everything in my life, three times. The day you were born. The day you died. And the day I found you again. You're still so present! My greatest teacher. I love you!

To every parent who has experienced child loss. May you know you are never alone on this journey, and our children are not gone. Just as my son is still here, so is your child. They are cheering you on, as am I. The hardest thing we will ever do is learn to live again, *with* them in a different way. Know you can do this, because you already are!

Table of Contents

Preface

My Son Died

"My son died. I am a bereaved parent." Words I never thought I'd say.

It's a club no one wants to belong to, yet I have been forced to join, just like every member before me. A cruel initiation into the life I must now figure out how to live.

I used to watch bereaved parents in awe. Now, I am the one being watched.

If you've lost a child, you know there are aspects of your loss you keep hidden. In life, we are taught to wear a mask, disguising emotion, only revealing what the world will deem acceptable.

The truth is, our loss terrifies them! It shines a light on just how fragile life is. No one is safe, not even a healthy child. Society will only allow themselves a brief peek into death's destruction before slamming the door shut. It's far too scary!

So, we wear our mask. There is a stigma attached. Mention the death of your child and an instant awkwardness floods the room. No one knows how to act or what to say. The look of pity is impossible to hide. Therefore, we try our best to avoid those conversations when we can.

Child loss is ugly, messy, and life changing; yet those words don't begin to do it justice. After a while, grief makes us feel like we have gone crazy, lost our minds.

Our entire lives are ripped away, leaving our arms empty, our bodies in shock, and our minds constantly searching. The dirty secret? None of us want to survive the loss of our child, not entirely.

While grief may be as individual as a fingerprint, there are many commonalities. Our survival sneaks up on us through the support of others who are like us. Hearing them share their stories of anger, hatred, yearning, crazy, and intense sorrow, builds an unbreakable bond. That bond helps us rise from the ash of destruction.

To survive, we must share our stories. The ugliness, the pain, and the truth of what it's like to outlive your own child. If we are honest, it's nothing like we thought it would be. It never is.

For those of us who share openly, there are still things we keep tucked away. Personal things too private to share, thoughts we are ashamed of, things we believe are just too far out there for someone else to understand yet, there is power in sharing.

When we pull back the curtain and allow the sunlight in, we shine a light into the darkness and achieve transparency, allowing others a raw look at what is real, giving others the opportunity to nod their head and say, "Me too!".

These moments change lives. They breed hope for the ability to survive. Most importantly, they reassure someone in the depths of despair they are not alone! That is powerful.

So, in an effort to pull back my curtain...

Our Story of Loss

My son went to bed a normal, excited Santa was on his way, hopeful that in the morning, he would find everything he wanted under the tree. He would have! I never would have guessed that 2 hours later, when he awoke sick, it would be the beginning of the end.

For a very long time, this night played on repeat in my mind. It still does, sometimes.

That Christmas Eve was just like any other before it. I was running down the list of all the things I still had to do: there were presents to wrap (every single one of them), reindeer food to make and sprinkle through the yard, a scheduled webcam with grandparents, and cookies to put out for Santa. There were not enough hours in the day, but I was counting down those hours to the kids' early bedtime.

The big kids, my son and my oldest daughter, sat at the kitchen table to decorate cookies for Santa. It was one of my "this will be a fun experience for them" projects that I always take on, then regret during execution. It was not so much the project, but that I would leave it go until the last hour and then try to cram everything in.

We snapped a few photos, and I ushered them away to clean up. We were going to crank these things out and get done so I wouldn't have to stay up all night wrapping gifts.

As the chaos eased, my son found himself on the couch in front of the TV. Out of the blue, he started complaining that his ear hurt. It wasn't just his normal kid complaint. He burst into tears, which was very out of character.

We discovered he had a very low-grade fever. I thought, "Great, an ear infection! It figures we'd end up with a sick kid for the holiday". It always seemed to happen this way. It was nearly 3 PM, so we hurried to get him to urgent care before they closed for the holiday at 6 PM. My husband took him.

Both ears were red and a little inflamed. He'd had a cough, so they prescribed him a Z-pack. I felt like we had checked another thing off the list.

They returned home that evening. He had picked out ginger ale and cheese popcorn at Walgreens for a snack later. He really hadn't eaten all day, so they stopped and grabbed McDonald's on the way home. Cameron was so excited, he ordered pancakes!

After dinner, his mood had perked up a bit. We took advantage of this and made our reindeer food. Reindeer have a very special place in our house. My son's favorite thing in the entire world was his stuffed reindeer. We have always made sure Santa's reindeer have a special treat. Oatmeal and marshmallows for eating. Glitter added so they can see the sparkle and know where to land. We sprinkled it all through the front yard.

Next was the webcam with my husband's parents. We don't live near family, so we found this was a great way for them to be incorporated into the holiday. We let the kids open their gifts from Grandma and Grandpa while they got to watch the fun.

I will never forget Cameron was mad at us! He didn't want to open any presents early. He wanted to save them all for Christmas morning. He gave in though, and I'm glad he did! The look of excitement on his face as he opened one of the video games he wanted. I wish I had taken more pictures.

He and our oldest daughter, Melia, took turns opening Sienna's presents (our youngest daughter). Almost immediately, Cameron asked if he could stay up and play his new game. I told him no. It was already getting late, and we had so much to do before morning. I wish I had let him.

To get him riled up, my husband joked that he would test the game out while Cameron slept that night, just to make sure it was going to work OK for him the next morning. He didn't find that funny.

Cameron asked if he could play in the morning before everyone else got up. I told him there was no way he was going to let us all sleep in on Christmas morning! He said it was OK, he wouldn't bother us, we could sleep a little while. Then we'd open presents later. The funny part is, I know he would have done just that.

Abruptly, Cameron stood up and announced he was tired, and he was going to bed. It was about 9 PM. Just like that, he picked up his games to take them with him (and keep his Dad from trying to play them), which made us chuckle, and off he went. I didn't get to tuck him in that night. He was asleep the moment his head hit the pillow.

We worked quickly to get Christmas ready. When the presents were wrapped and under the tree, it was still early so we decided to watch a movie. I was listening carefully for either of the big kids to get out of bed. I didn't want them coming in to see the tree before morning.

We were no more than 15 minutes into the movie when I heard movement. It was now 11 PM. Someone was up. I sprinted to their side of the house to intercept and found Cameron in his bathroom, sick. He was sitting on the toilet as I shoved the trash can into his hands. A mess surrounded him.

I frantically yelled for my husband to grab the bucket and started shouting out all the things I needed to clean up.

I thought, "Great, that damn stomach bug is back." We had battled it two weeks prior.

When the vomiting had stopped, the first words out of his mouth were, "Has Santa been here yet?" He was so sweet. I lied and told him no. I said it was still too early. As I cleaned up the bathroom floor, he got into the shower to get washed up.

We got him settled on the couch, in the area off the kitchen. He was all comfy with the bucket at his side. We sat at the table behind him, so we could be close. Every time he moved or made a sound, I would jump up to check on him and see if he was going to be sick.

His fever had gone up to 101. We attempted Tylenol; but almost immediately, he was sick again. He was thirsty and would ask for a small sip of water, which produced the same result. He had even lost control of his bladder.

By this time, it was almost 1 AM. I carried him into the bathroom. He was so tired and weak that he couldn't walk on his own. My mind screamed at me, "This is weird. This stuff isn't normal."

I sat him down on the toilet and began cleaning him up. He tried to talk to me. I don't recall what he was trying to say, just that he had slurred a couple of words and seemed to struggle. His response times were a little slower than usual. Then he said, "It looks like everything is turning into Legos."

At this point, Cameron could no longer stand on his own. My husband had to hold him up in the shower to get him cleaned up yet again. Things felt really off.

My husband kept telling me that surely it was just because he was so tired. I knew he was, but it just didn't make sense to me. He should have been able to rally more than he had. Call it mother's intuition, but I knew there was something more going on.

We got him settled back on the couch. Our watch resumed. Apparently, I was too attentive because he opened his eyes and glared at me. He harshly whispered, "You just woke me up Mom. I was sleeping." It struck me as odd because it was so out of character for him to speak to me like this.

He began asking for water again because he was so thirsty. We took his temperature. 103.5. It was time for the ER. We weren't able to control his temperature. I was sure he was going to need an IV for medicine and fluids. It was now 2:30 AM.

We stood there looking at each other, mentally drawing straws to see who would draw the short end. It was me. My husband had taken him to urgent care. I got the hospital, for which I am now forever grateful.

I ran to pull on clothes and make myself presentable. My husband gathered our things and carried him to the car. We put him in the front seat with me, buckled him in, and he held the bucket.

On our way there, he commented on the number of green lights we were hitting and how lucky we were. I just kept thinking we'd be OK once we arrived at the hospital.

Just as we were turning the corner into the ER, I asked him if we needed to take the bucket in with us. He said no. I asked him if he felt like he was going to be sick again. He said no. No sooner did he say it, he was throwing up again.

I pulled up to the ER door, ran inside, grabbed a wheelchair, lifted him into it, and placed the bucket beside him. As I wheeled him in, they took him immediately to the back to take his vitals. By the time I returned from parking the car, we were being wheeled to a bed.

They tried to administer Tylenol. He still couldn't keep it down. They started an IV. He barely flinched. In spite of all the fluids, he kept asking for water because he was so thirsty. I have no idea what his temperature was at that point.

The tests began: first a round of blood work and chest X-rays.

I went with him for the X-rays. They wanted him to sit up on the side of his bed against the board. I had to hold him up because he couldn't do it on his own. The technician asked me if he was always like this. I could tell she knew this wasn't normal, even given how sick he was. She predicted we would see her again soon and that they would be asking for a CT scan. She was right.

Back in the room, everyone that came in would ask him how he was feeling. He always responded with a weak, "Good." I kept telling him he needed to stop saying good. That he needed to tell us how he really felt so we could figure out what was wrong and fix it. He would then say, "I'm dizzy." He never offered more.

The nurse brought him a little present. She told him he could open it now or save it for when he felt a little better. He turned it around in his hands, inspecting it. He then told her he wanted to save it, so he could open it on Christmas. She asked if he knew what day it was. By this time, it was already

Christmas. It didn't matter to him. He held onto that present because he intended to open it with the rest of his gifts later.

I sat in a chair near the end of his bed. My eyes shifted between him and my phone. I had been texting updates to my husband and my mom, trying to distract myself with scrolling. He kept trying to fall asleep. It would never last long, however. We had so many people in our room. It was a constant stream, coming in and going out.

Test results had started to come in. I don't even know everything they were testing for. Most were normal, some were a little strange. The medical mystery had begun.

Things took a sharp turn as they began to question me about him drinking alcohol. The tone shifted, and I suddenly felt like I was on trial. No matter how much I told them there was 100% no chance, I felt like no one believed me. We don't drink. We don't have alcohol in our house. My son was a big rule follower, and even if we had it in the house, he never would have taken a drink, even if he'd been pressured to try it.

The game was changing. The doctors had no idea what was happening!

We also had his CT scan results. One doctor said, "We see a small area with some swelling, but nothing to be concerned about." They seemed confident it was either encephalitis or meningitis; yet he stood over Cameron and kept asking questions. I could tell he was looking for clues as to what he needed to do next.

This was about the time a thought flashed into my head. In my thought, I questioned whether my son would even survive. In that moment, I was so angry at myself for even thinking it. I shoved it out of my brain, refusing to dwell on it. I continued telling myself we had to be close to figuring it out. Once we did, I was sure we'd be on the road to recovery.

The doctor had left and quickly returned to tell me they wanted to admit him. He said we were going to be transported to the children's hospital, which was downtown. Our doctor was having regular conversations with their ICU doctor to make sure they were running the right tests and not missing anything. Our next test would be a spinal tap.

In the middle of this conversation, Cameron sat straight up and asked me if I would help him. I asked what he needed. He asked if I would help buckle him. I said, "What?" He asked if I could help him get buckled in the car. I told him we weren't in the car and asked if he knew where we were. He looked around and said yes, we were at the hospital. I told him he didn't need to be buckled, that he could just lie back and try to rest.

The doctor asked me if he had been saying strange things like that all night. I told him he had, off and on, since becoming sick.

Finally, I felt like someone was seeing what I was seeing. Maybe they would take me seriously now?

After a moment, Cameron opened his eyes and looked at me. I will never forget the look in his eyes, because it was nothing

I had ever seen before! I asked him if he was OK. He said yes. I asked him if he was scared. He said no. I said, "I love you." He said, "I love you". Then, he closed his eyes again.

This was the last lucid moment I had with my son. I really think he knew what was coming. This was his way of trying to make it OK for me.

By this time, it was nearing 6 AM. Cameron had settled in and started to sleep a bit. I didn't want to bother him. The doctor came in and we were preparing for the spinal tap. He attempted to wake Cameron to explain what they were going to do next.

We couldn't wake him. His eyes would open, but he would only stare off in the distance before closing them again. The doctor and I both took turns shaking him, calling his name, trying anything to wake him. Nothing worked.

I didn't know it at the time, but this was the last time he would ever be conscious.

We were now being whisked into a larger room. There were now at least a dozen doctors and nurses with us. Another IV was being started in his arm. He was quickly being prepped for the spinal tap.

My poor boy just lay lifeless on the bed, like a little rag doll.

A shift change in the ER had begun, as new people were coming into the room to get updates and take over. This changeover was my mental realization it had to be around 7 AM.

The nurse who entered took her place by his side and asked why he still had his t-shirt on. She seemed annoyed and grabbed her scissors. She quickly turned and asked me if it was OK to cut the shirt. I just nodded and told her to do whatever she needed to do.

I felt so small as I stood in the corner of the room. It was one of those moments in a movie where things are rapidly happening around you, but the sound fades away, and you just see it all in slow motion. I had a clear view to watch everything. I was completely helpless.

The nurse was talking to him, telling him what they were doing as they prepped him for his spinal tap. She rolled him to his side, and they held him still, though their efforts didn't matter because there was no reaction from him. It seemed to take forever.

The ambulance team had arrived from the children's hospital. They all kept telling me things were OK. His vitals were stable. He was "emergent", but they were taking good care of him.

There was hollering back and forth as everyone demanded the results. This number was supposed to determine if he had encephalitis or meningitis.

It was not meningitis. Maybe this meant we had an answer? I needed to hear that we had an answer.

I watched him seize a few times. His little toes curled up hard and his hands balled into fists. No one else seemed to take notice. Did that mean it was expected? Not a big deal? It felt like a big deal. How did we get here?

The decision was made to intubate him for the ambulance ride. It was precautionary so that he wouldn't stop breathing en route to the hospital. It all seemed incredibly surreal. This was supposed to be a "quick trip" to the hospital, maybe an overnight stay, but that was it.

Again, it took forever!

I knew this was my only chance to run to the car. I had to leave his clothes, minus the t-shirt they had cut off him and our bucket, covered in what looked like coffee grounds. I didn't want to carry these items with me to our next destination. So, I ran as fast as I could to the car and back.

As he was loaded into the back of the ambulance, the nurse who had been caring for him came to give me a hug. She told me she wanted me to bring him back to see her when this was all over and he was better. I promised I would. She had been amazing!

I had to ride in the front of the ambulance. The normal 25-minute drive felt like it took hours. The sound of sirens will never be the same!

The EMT driving the ambulance did his best to engage me in conversation. I can't tell you what we talked about. I was more aware of the fact that cars didn't move out of our way like they should, which slowed us down. I was also keenly aware that he was distracted by the video monitor showing him what was happening in the back.

By the time we pulled into the parking lot of the children's hospital, things had changed. As I climbed out of the ambulance, I was being told there were new plans. One of the EMTs had said Cameron's pupils had stopped responding during transit. He said they had to "do a couple of things"; therefore, instead of going to the ICU step-down unit, we were going directly to a CT scan, then to Pediatric ICU.

I followed them like a lost little puppy as we navigated through the halls of the hospital. I wasn't allowed into the CT scan area, so I stood in the hallway, frantically trying to send a text message to update my husband.

As the door opened, they wheeled him out, and we continued our journey to the 2nd floor PICU.

When we arrived at the room, there were already a handful of nurses and doctors there to meet us. I was swarmed as residents began asking me a million questions. Others were diving in to evaluate him and get him hooked up to their machines. Then, I found myself standing in the background again, watching, analyzing faces, praying; and I don't pray.

The doctor had her back to me. She appeared young but was in command of the room.

Things were frantic, like during his spinal tap. The doctor was working quickly to assess the situation. She was yelling at nurses to go gather as much epinephrine as they could get. I remember her telling them to break the rules if they had to because she knew their restrictions and red tape would take too much time. You could feel the electricity in the room, with everyone poised on the edge of their seat, waiting for those CT results.

The doctor took out her cell phone and called down to Imaging. She told the person on the other end to pull the CT results as fast as they could and to call her back. She handed her phone to someone else in the room, their only job was to answer it.

No more than a few minutes had passed when the phone rang. The woman holding the doctor's cell phone immediately answered.

I will never forget that look in her eyes as she made eye contact with the doctor. It was an intense sadness, one that made me realize things were worse than I could have ever imagined. She handed the phone to the doctor and exchanged worried looks. As the doctor stepped into the hall, she asked, "How bad is it?"

When she returned, she took a seat next to me at the back of the room. I was anxious to hear any updates and braced for the worst.

She explained that his CT scan looked really bad. His brain was so swollen it had started to expand into his spinal cavity. She stressed she was very concerned about everything she was seeing. That she had called in a neurosurgeon consult to look at his scans and see if there was anything that could be done.

Once again, I found myself focusing in on the behaviors before me. It struck me that she was being so careful with her words so as not to give me any hope, only facts. She was strategic in only sharing a small portion of what she knew in that moment. She told me they were going to need to start a central line in his femoral artery. It needed to be done in a sterile environment, so I would have to leave the room.

As we exited the room and began walking down the hall to a waiting area, I burst into tears. They exploded from deep inside me, out of nowhere. It was the first time I had let myself cry or feel any ounce of emotion; but I was immediately angry with myself. I needed to stay in control, because if there was any chance in hell that my boy would open his eyes again, I needed to be right there to reassure him everything would be OK. There was no way I could let him see me a mess.

I don't recall how long I was out of his room, though I do remember watching a clock on the wall. I must have been aware of the time, to some extent, because my mind had drifted to the idea that if we had been at home, had this day gone according to plan, the kids would have already opened their gifts. We would have been enjoying the day, Christmas day, my birthday.

We had reached the stage where I knew my husband needed to get to the hospital. I began trying to track down childcare. We had no family near us. How do you call people on Christmas morning and ask them to leave their family festivities to take care of your kids so your husband can come to the hospital?

Somehow, I did get lucky. A friend picked up her phone. She dropped everything, canceled plans with her family, and rushed to my house.

I had family telling me they were making calls to get on a plane. Things felt again like they were escalating too quickly. I kept telling them to wait. We didn't even have a diagnosis yet. In my heart I knew if they were coming, it meant things really were as bad as they seemed.

I paced the hallway. I kept telling myself to be patient. Everything they had done earlier took ten times longer than expected. This would too. I was anxious to get back into that room.

I looked up as two doctors walked down the hall toward me, their faces were blank. I knew, in my gut, I was about to receive the news every parent feared.

They led me to a conference room and closed the door. Our doctor asked me if there was family they could call. I told her my husband was on his way, but I wasn't sure how far away he was. She asked if I wanted her to wait, or if she should come back and talk to him when he arrived. I just wanted the update.

She explained again the horrible CT results. She told me the neurosurgeon reviewed all his tests, including the assumed normal CT scan we had had just three hours earlier. There was nothing the neurosurgeon could do. The swelling was far too great. His brain was gravely injured from stroke, swelling, and infection. The areas of his brain that were impacted greatest were those that controlled things he needed to live, like heart rate and breathing. She explained that even if he came out of this, the parts of him that made him Cameron would be gone.

It wasn't until I had asked her for what the odds were that he could wake up that it really sunk in and hit me. She told me is he had seen many things in medicine she could not explain, but she did not expect him to make it.

In that moment, my heart broke! How was I supposed to accept that? How was I supposed to even think about life without this little boy? It wasn't fair!

They told me I was allowed to go back to the room. I couldn't get to him fast enough. I had no idea what would come next. I was in complete shock and didn't think to ask.

Cameron was being put into isolation because we still didn't know the cause of his illness. Everyone who came into the room had to gear up in gowns, hats, and masks… except me. The testing continued because they were still looking for clues and answers.

When my husband, David, arrived with Cameron's reindeer in hand, I had to deliver the news. We cried.

The doctor returned and sat with us at the back of the room. She explained everything to David, just as she had done for me.

This was the first time I thought about our girls at home. Poor Melia, who was four at the time, was still waiting for us to return home from the hospital so she could open Christmas presents.

We struggled with what to do. We knew we had family jumping on planes to get to us. It felt like the entire world was descending upon us and we were losing control. We needed to be able to tell Melia the news before anyone else arrived. They would be filled with their own emotions and would cause more confusion for her.

We knew our only option was to make the trek home and tell her in person. It was devastatingly hard to leave Cameron at the hospital, alone. The only reason we felt we could leave was because we knew if he was standing there, he would have told us to leave him and go home to tell the girls. So, we did.

We made the 45 minute drive home. I had no idea what we were going to say, even as we pulled into the driveway. The moment I saw her, I just started crying! She asked me what was wrong and gave me a big hug.

I explained to her how sick Cameron was, that his brain was sick, that he was sleeping, that the doctors had told us he wouldn't be able to wake up, and that he wouldn't be able to come home.

She tried to ignore what I was saying and asked to open presents. So, we did. She deserved that.

She loved the 1-on-1 attention as I sat next to her on the floor and tried hard to smile. She told me she was so glad it was just her, Daddy, and I. Those words stung, though she didn't understand why. To her, this was just time outside of her brother's shadow. I held back a flood of tears.

When we finished unwrapping, we told her we had to go back to the hospital. She was OK with that because she was having so much fun with my friend, Penny. Penny was a godsend that day! I could never thank her enough for giving up her Christmas plans to watch the girls until our family arrived!

The drive back to the hospital took forever.

As we exited the parking garage and prepared to enter the building, we were met by my uncle, who wrapped us in a big hug. He lived three hours away and got in his car to make the drive as soon as he heard. Our own protective bubble had burst. People knew. They were coming.

There were no updates or changes when we arrived back in Cameron's room. He was freezing cold, so they brought in heated blankets to warm him. Looking back now, I'm sure that had been for me more than it was for him.

The medical mystery just seemed to grow. All they could tell us was they thought maybe it was encephalitis. That it was possibly a virus. If so, we all likely had it. For the rest of us, it was a cold. For him, however, it had attacked his brain.

Nothing they said resonated or made sense.

I couldn't tell you how many people had told me they had never seen deterioration happen so quickly! They had also told us they would continue to search for answers, so we would have closure and know the actual cause of Cameron's illness. In case you were wondering, there is no closure with child loss.

David held onto the hope that Cameron would open his eyes, that they'd find something, or that they'd be able to do something. I kept telling him not to go there. It wasn't that I didn't want to have hope, but I told him they had explained to me there wasn't hope.

I just stood beside Cameron's bed and held his hand. I don't think David really got to my stage of understanding until the nurses allowed me to get into bed with Cameron. He had his favorite toy, Reindeer, tucked under one arm, and I laid beside him, trying not to disrupt the tubes and needles.

I will never forget the cold of his forehead on my lips.

The tests continued. No answers.

The doctor explained the process of determining brain death, because that's what would come next. They would perform a series of tests, checking for pupil response, reflexes, and pain. These could only be started after he had been admitted for 12 hours. We would then have to wait an additional 12 hours and have a second doctor complete the same set of tests, with the same outcome. It was all so surreal.

She then put the power into our hands. She told us we could delay that process as long as we wanted, and the decision on when to begin the first round was ours.

From this point on, we waited for death.

The thought that it could come on its own had never really crossed my mind. However, I knew doctors had to keep increasing his medication to elevate his blood pressure. It had already been increased several times throughout the day because his heart rate kept dropping.

I laid there, next to him, watching him breathe (artificially), memorizing his features, his freckles, everything. My body was so tired, as I had been awake for 36 hours, but I willed myself to stay awake. I couldn't waste a single moment sleeping when I knew these were his final moments. I had to be present.

The Aerosmith song "I Don't Want to Miss a Thing" entered my mind.[1]

I could stay awake just to hear you breathing
Watch you smile while you are sleeping
While you're far away and dreaming
I could spend my life in this sweet surrender
I could stay lost in this moment forever
Every moment spent with you is a moment I treasure
Don't want to close my eyes
I don't want to fall asleep
'Cause I'd miss you, babe
And I don't want to miss a thing.

---

[1] I DON'T WANT TO MISS A THING
Words and Music by DIANE WARREN
© 1998 REALSONGS (ASCAP)
All Rights Reserved
Used by Permission of ALFRED MUSIC

By 8:30 PM, our immediate family had all arrived.

There were hugs in the hallway as everyone had on their brave face. They took turns gearing up to go in and see Cameron. Decisions were made about who would go relieve my friend of her childcare duties and take over the care of our daughters.

My only focus was staying with Cameron.

We asked the doctor to begin her first round of testing as soon as she could. By this time, it was 10 PM. David and I both felt like delaying it was the wrong thing to do. We knew what the outcome was going to be. It wasn't fair to Cameron to be kept alive by all these machines any longer than was necessary.

At 10:10, the doctor came in for the first round of brain activity tests. We were told we could stay in the room if we wanted. I wasn't leaving! David struggled with it, but stayed. For me, it didn't matter what they were doing. Cameron wasn't going to be alone. So, we stood together at the foot of the bed.

The results were as we had expected. His brain was no longer functioning. He was brain dead.

This was the first time we asked the doctor what we could do. We stopped her before she left the room, because we couldn't stand the thought of waiting another 12 hours to do it all again with the same result. She told us their plan was to continue to increase the heart meds as needed. We asked if we could skip this intervention. She explained to us that legally they had to perform the second round of testing;

however, she wanted to consult with some other doctors to see what we could do medically.

Only a few minutes had passed before she returned. She had a solution. As long as we had three attending physicians in the room, in agreement with the situation, we could make all of the decisions and do it on our own terms. She said there were already two of them on board. The third doctor was in their car, on the way to the hospital, to weigh in on the situation.

We took it.

As soon as everyone was there, we were given paperwork to sign. Once again, the timetable was ours. When we were ready, we just had to let them know. We didn't wait.

Looking back, I don't know how we made the decision we did. If I could go back, I would have probably stalled for more time to memorize him, but I was so exhausted, mentally, emotionally, and physically. We really were making the best decision for him. That's what parents should do, right?!

I can't tell you who was in the room with us. All of my attention was on my boy.

Slowly, they began decreasing his heart meds. I just laid in bed with him and held him. I kept whispering that it was OK. That I loved him and would miss him so much.

He and I had had several conversations about death, so we had talked a lot about what we would do when one of us arrived in heaven. He had always said if he got there before me, he would meet up with our dog, Max, and then he would wait for me to get there. How was it possible this was the scenario that would play out?

I consciously watched his chest. It was important to me to see him take his last breath. Something I would never forget.

He died at 12:19 on December 26th.

He waited. You see, Christmas is also my birthday. I believe he waited so that it didn't happen on my birthday.

From that moment forward, the question I continue to ask myself is, "What do I do now?" I'm not sure if that will ever change. It was so incredibly hard to leave the room that night, to walk away from his body lying in that hospital bed. It just felt so final. It was.

It was the last time I ever saw my son's body.

The following week would be the hardest of my life. How does a person move on from losing a child?

My favorite boy was gone. I still didn't have answers.

…..

It took 7 months to get those answers.

Chapter 1

The Beginning of After

What have we done?

My very first thought in what will forever be known as "after".

It wasn't regret in the decisions we made, because we really didn't have control over those choices. They were essentially happening whether we intervened or not. I know in my head and my heart that we made all the right decisions based on the information we had in each moment. Yet, I felt responsible for the devastation of his life… of our life.

How did we get here? My son was healthy and then spiraled out of control in a matter of 12 hours. Every parent's worst nightmare, but now it was our reality.

I can't tell you how many times I had wished I would wake up and it would all be just a bad dream.

I needed a re-do button. Something, *anything* that would let me go back and do things over again for the opportunity at a different outcome. I felt a kind of desperation I had never felt before. A need to be able to do something, but with the full understanding that nothing – *nothing* - could ever fix this.

That kind of desperation is hard to put into words. It is agonizing on a soul level.

The walk out of the hospital took every ounce of focus and control I had. It felt like no one could see the internal turmoil I felt. No one else appeared fixated on what we were leaving behind. It was as if I was in this bubble, where the entire world was moving around me, and inside, the silence was deafening, and everything was frozen.

I wanted nothing more than to run back into that room and crawl back into his bed. If I'm being honest, one of my deepest regrets is that I didn't.

Seeing him in that bed through the window… so small… all by himself; and I was just leaving, walking away like none of it mattered, leaving him there, never to be seen again. *Never.*

That thought will send me into a tailspin over and over if I go there. So, I won't.

I blacked out the entire ride home.

Waking up that first morning, the entire world felt different. There was a heavy, tangible shift in energy. It is a feeling I will never forget. Somehow, everything seemed the same; but nothing was.

I'm convinced his first sign came that morning. I just wasn't in a place to fully recognize it yet.

I felt someone lean ever so gently into the side of my bed, right at my shoulder, exactly the way he would wake me in the mornings. My eyes popped open as my heart started to race. I fully expected to see him standing there beside me as he always had… but nothing. The room was empty. It felt like a cruel joke.

I remember grabbing my phone to check the time. It was just after 6 AM. Exactly the time he used to show up. Had I imagined it?! It had felt so real. I *know* I had felt it! But grief can make us feel crazy. I didn't know then what I believe now.

I lay there in bed, staring at the doorway he used to walk through to wake me, but never would again. The heavy realization that he was no longer physically in our world was a shock.

Our house was full of people. People I didn't want to come in the first place, because their act of showing up meant everything we were experiencing was real.

I just wanted to create a bubble and shut everyone else outside of it. A quiet space where it was just me and Cameron, and I didn't have to let anyone else in.

Unfortunately, life doesn't work like that. These fantasies stay just that, fantasies. So, I found myself climbing out of bed to make sure my daughters were being cared for. I knew they were, but I guess it was habit.

Opening that bedroom door to this new world was a sensory overload I didn't expect.

He should be standing on that spot in front of the TV, jumping up and down while playing his video games. That's how I should have been greeted; but I wasn't.

I entered the kitchen, as people paused what they were doing and raised their eyes to look at me. I felt the room go quiet as they searched for words and signs of my state of mind.

I kept walking.

I realized the dog was following me because she hadn't been out yet. Yes, an escape! My saving grace, until I opened the patio door and it hit me: the reason she hadn't been out yet was because my son was no longer there to take her out as he did each morning.

My pace quickened as I slid out of the patio area to hide around the corner of the house where no one could see me break down, head in my hands, and sob.

How was this my reality? What am I supposed to do now?

I honestly don't remember a lot of what happened in those first few weeks. The thick fog of grief had settled in and clouded my mind.

No one told us what came next. We were just asked to sign some papers at the hospital, and we were sent home to navigate this loss on our own. If it hadn't been for my mom telling us we needed to find a funeral home, I would have walked in a fog until the hospital called, wondering what to do with his body.

How were we expected to do this alone? Our world had been turned upside down. I just needed someone to hand me a list and say, "Start here. I got you." That list didn't seem to exist.

What really stood out to me in "the after" is that the world kept spinning and spinning. People kept on living their lives as if nothing changed. But everything had changed! My bearings were lost. Nothing made sense. I needed it all to stop so I could breathe, catch up, and process what happened.

I didn't want to be here… in "the after".

The entire world looked and felt different. I hated it. Though, hate is not a strong enough word for how it really felt. I would soon find there were a lot of words in the English language that weren't strong enough and didn't do my grief justice.

I was being forced to live a life I didn't want, didn't choose. Everything was out of my control, and I was just expected to keep going like it was all OK. But nothing was going to be OK again.

Child loss changes you to your core. Things that once made sense, no longer do. Your entire being is preoccupied, distracted, existing in a haze that feels like an alternate universe. Their death defines you, consumes you.

One thing I do remember is how his final days played on repeat in my head. Eyes open, eyes closed, it didn't matter. It was all I saw – all I thought about – over and over again.

The moments that lead up to your child's death burn into your memory, shatter your heart, traumatize your soul. Like a movie reel on repeat, they play over and over in your mind.

These are mine:

7 Is Too Young To Die[2]

This was it. The moment I was dreading. The end. As I lay there in his hospital bed, holding him, I focused all of my attention on his chest. As the machine pumped, I could see it rise, then fall. I tuned in to the sound, blocking everything else out, waiting. I never turned my eyes away. I didn't want to miss his last breath.

I whispered into his ear, "It's OK. We will be OK. Don't worry. I love you."

Out of the corner of my eye, I saw the nurse move to turn off the last machine. I kept my eyes on his chest. Up. Down. That was it. It felt anticlimactic. I held on for just a few more minutes. Lips pressed to his forehead. Memorizing him and how he felt in my arms.

As I let go, I told myself he was gone. He was no longer in this body that lay before me. Yet, I couldn't take my eyes off

---

[2] Graham, E. (2017). *7 Is Too Young To Die*. Her View From Home. https://herviewfromhome.com/7-is-too-young-to-die/.

him. All I kept thinking was, "Look at what we just did." As if we had had any control over the events of the day or this gut-wrenching outcome. It didn't seem real.

Seven is too young! How am I supposed to live without him?

The room cleared out. To be honest, I had forgotten anyone else was still there. I blocked them out, trying to absorb every last moment I had with my son. "No regrets," I had told myself.

Twenty minutes went by. It felt like an eternity. I was exhausted and had been awake the last 48-hours. We were still waiting for the final paperwork. Why it hadn't been prepared before they had turned him off, I will never understand.

What would come next? We had no clue! The disorganization made me angry. Why did they make me sit here and look at what we had done?! This was so wrong. In spite of my anger, I kept quiet. All I could do was look at him.

As I sat in the chair, beside the body of my dead son, I will never forget the paleness of his skin. I watched as white spots started to appear on his hands as the blood drained away. How his chest was no longer rising, as it had done earlier. I had to keep reminding myself that he wasn't in there anymore, so it was OK.

As we stood in the hallway, ready to leave, I looked back at him through the window. He looked so helpless…so small in that big room. The urge to go back in and hug him was overwhelming. To be honest, I really wanted to climb back into his bed and never leave it. He was my baby boy. Someone needed to stay with him and make sure he was OK. How could I just leave him? It wasn't right. That feeling stayed with me the entire car ride home. A big part of me died that night.

Life is cruel in ways you can never imagine. It was Christmas Day and my birthday. Here we were, unexpectedly ending the life of my oldest child, my favorite boy. My two girls were at home, being robbed of their brother and the joy of this holiday. It just wasn't fair.

He went to bed on Christmas Eve, a normal, healthy boy. When he awoke 2 hours later, he was sick. Not the kind of sick that makes you think anything really serious is going on, just a stomach bug and a fever. Even when we put him in the car 3 hours later for the ER, there was no expectation that this would turn out as it did. In my head, our worst-case scenario was a brief hospital stay. Yet somehow, in just under 12 hours, we were being told he wasn't going to make it. How was that possible?!

We lived every parent's worst nightmare...on Christmas. Our favorite holiday, now forever impacted by tragedy. My birthday, forever changed. Our family dynamic and function would never be the same!

I always thought the hardest part would be turning off that machine and leaving the hospital. I was wrong! The hardest part came after. In those moments, when the numbness briefly wore off, when I realized I am still living – we were still living, and he was no longer there, and there was nothing to be done to fix it.

It's a daily struggle. Our house is quiet, though it's not. His spot is empty. It is a spot only he can fill. Everywhere I look, I am reminded of him. Nothing is the same. It never will be again.

People often use the word strong. I don't see strength. I see bare minimum, fulfillment of obligation. Doing what we need to do to survive. A slow push to rebuild to something that resembles normal, even though I don't want a new normal. People want to help. They mean well. To them, it's important to see us doing well, to see us surviving and moving forward. So, we put on a brave smile and appear to do just that.

Someday, maybe we will look back and realize that we have succeeded. Until then, our happiness exists in our before. Everything else is after.

Chapter 2

I Knew Six Years Before It Happened

"You will lose a child."

I vividly remember walking out of the bedroom into the loft area of our 2-story home as I heard the voice say these words. I stopped in my tracks, completely taken aback and shocked.

What had just happened? Was this real? My mind struggled to process.

It wasn't an actual voice I heard. More like a voice inside my head. Yet, it wasn't mine. It was different. This thought, I knew, didn't originate from anywhere inside of me.

I glanced into the corner of the room at Cameron. He wasn't quite two years old. I watched as he played with his toys. Why would those words pop into my mind at that moment? What a horrible thing to think! Where did it come from?

I was filled with guilt and shame for even allowing myself to think it. Yet, it wasn't me.

Like every other parent, the idea of losing a child was my worst nightmare. Yet, I did what everyone else does. I thought, "That won't happen to us."

However, in the back of my mind, I was terrified.

It took me a few minutes, but I shook it off. I never spoke of it to anyone. Yet, the experience haunted me and was never far from my thoughts. Why? Because I had heard that voice once before… and what it said had come true.

This is going to sound crazy, but…

It's a phrase I find myself repeating over and over on this grief walk.

This voice began almost 20 years earlier, while I was in college…

It was the summer after my freshman year. As a small-town girl, my life was full of sensible, secure choices. I had moved just a few hours away to attend college. I followed and was engaged to my high school sweetheart. There was a plan for a good life. A future filled with all the things society and those around me told me I should have and want.

However, I was feeling suffocated by the safety net I had built around me. Something was missing. It wasn't that I was unhappy. I was searching for something more. Maybe I was just looking for me.

I decided to do something big – something scary.

I accepted an internship that would take me to the other side of the country, where I would live in a big city, all by myself. I was testing the waters. I needed to see if I could stand on my own two feet, alone.

I remember immediately hitting it off with my suite mate. One of our first days in the dorm was spent in her room, talking. I hadn't met many others in the program yet. A group of them had gone to dinner the night before, and she began sharing the highlights.

As she ran down the list of names and shared her impressions, I was busying myself around the room, making lunch.

She said, "Have you met David yet?"

"No, not yet." I replied.

As she said, "I think you'll really like him," it happened.

I heard a voice say, "This is the guy you will marry."

Immediately, I froze. She kept talking.

Standing in front of a mirror, my head snapped up. I remember looking myself in the eye, wondering what the hell had just happened. Where did that voice come from? What a crazy thing to just randomly think about a complete stranger! Plus, I was engaged. What was wrong with me?!

I never told anyone about it, but it rattled me and left an imprint.

At the end of the summer, I found myself ending my engagement. My big, scary decision to go out into the world had made me realize I no longer wanted that safe, small-town life. Shortly after, David and I started a long-distance relationship.

Six years would pass before we were officially engaged, planning to be married.

But the voice was right.

I was reminded repeatedly

As my son grew up, I found myself being very intentional in remembering moments. It's something I have never experienced with my other children. I used to chalk it up to him being my first born. As I look back, I'm not convinced it was only that. I believe it was because something in me knew I would need these moments. So, I memorized vivid mental pictures.

The phrase "nothing lasts forever" would ring in my ears often. As milestones came and went, I took this constant message as my brain telling me he's growing up. Nothing more. Still, I would pause, take a mental snapshot, and think of that day.

The voice was different during these milestones, maybe just less shocking. It sounded more like me. I was able to disregard it and believe it was just the normal thoughts of a mother with a strong awareness her little boy wouldn't be little forever.

These messages intensified in his last year. As did my feelings of being crazy.

One night, I went into his room, as I always did, to turn off the overhead light and switch on his lamp before bed. He insisted on having the lights on to go to sleep. As the light dimmed, I turned to leave, pausing for a moment to watch him sleep.

My mind triggered, "Remember this moment. It won't last long."

Again, I reconciled it as him getting older.

I took another mental snapshot. I remember this night like it was yesterday.

That Special Bond Between Mother and Son[3]

Standing in the low light of his room, I pause for a moment. Studying the shadows that drape across his sweet little face. He looks so peaceful as he sleeps.

I feel my heart beat a little faster. My chest fills with warmth, butterflies stir in my stomach, and love overflows from every pore. I swear my heart could literally explode. My only thought, "Wow! I am so in love with this little boy."

I reach down and scooped Reindeer up off the floor. At seven, I'm not sure if he really needs Reindeer as much as I want him to still need Reindeer. Regardless, I tuck him gently into the covers beside my favorite boy. He's growing up so fast.

Unable to move, I stand there and take it all in. Overwhelmed by my love for him, I just want to squeeze

---

[3] Graham, E. (2017). *That Special Bond Between Mother And Son*. Her View From Home. https://herviewfromhome.com/that-special-bond-between-mother-and-son/.

him! I hear myself say, "I never thought it was possible to love someone so much."

My thoughts begin to wander. I try to imagine the type of person he will fall in love with someday. What their relationship will be like. Immediately I hear, "There's no way that person could ever love you as much as I do!"

It's in this moment that I realize somewhere deep inside of me there is a monster-in-law awakening. To be honest, I'm a bit surprised. Immediately, I promise myself I won't be one of those mothers who never thinks anyone is good enough for their son. Or, at least if I do, I will hide it deep down inside me, somewhere. I will vow now to love whomever he chooses to love. The most important thing is always his happiness in life.

Then, I realize how crazy I sound. Love really makes us crazy!

Before I became a mom, I had no concept of how my life would change. The depth in which I could feel love and the intensity of the attachment that would develop between us. I think back to the day the doctor told me it was a boy. I regret the brief moment of disappointment that crossed my mind, even though I had said all I wanted was a healthy baby. I just had no idea what I was going to do with a boy. Those feelings quickly faded into excitement. A new adventure that would change everything in the best possible way.

Almost eight years later, I am in awe of how much he has taught me about life. There is just something so special about a mother-son bond: so pure, unconditional, and beautifully sweet. I often wonder how I got so lucky? This little boy made me a mom. His mere existence made me complete.

.....

It happened again a short time later.

My son and daughter had asked to sleep in my room. For whatever reason, this had become a special treat. We made their beds on the floor.

Sometime after the giggles and hushed whispers faded, my son climbed into my bed.

I found him sleeping peacefully next to my spot. Knowing my husband would move him back to his bed on the floor, I let him stay awhile and slid in beside him.

I watched his chest rise and fall. Only half of his face was visible above the pillows. His hand lay stretched out on top of the blankets between us. I felt an overwhelming desire to hold his hand. My hand scooped underneath and cradled his hand in mine as I watched him sleep.

In my head I heard, "This won't last forever". I knew it was right. He was getting older. Before long, he wouldn't want to sleep in my bed. I would cherish the moments I had left before he grows up.

I took another mental snapshot.

The next time I heard the voice, it was mere weeks before Cameron died.

It was bedtime. Like any normal, frazzled mother at the end of a long day, I was rushing the kids through our routine. No books or extended snuggle sessions. It was a quick hug and kiss, followed by lights out.

Cameron was always the last stop, as he was oldest. When I arrived, he was flopped out on his bed, reading his latest *Magic Treehouse* book. As I entered the room, I said, "It's bedtime. Put the book away."

He turned his head to excitedly share whatever adventure was currently underway, hoping to pique my interest enough to garner some extra reading time. I started prepping his room, like I always did. He begged for me to sit next to him, so he could read the rest of the chapter to me.

Clear as day, I heard, "There isn't much time left."

The exact phrasing of it struck me as odd. It felt different. The voice was probably right. It wouldn't be long, and Cameron would no longer ask me to lie beside him in bed or listen to him read.

Instead of rushing through the rest of bedtime, I flopped down beside him. While I don't recall exactly what he read, I will never forget how we giggled and talked. When we were done, I tucked him into bed.

My brain took another mental snapshot.

The final time I heard the voice, I was standing over his hospital bed. This is the story I mentioned I would come back to later.

We were almost 4 hours into his sudden illness. We had been escorted back to a room in the ER. I stood at the end of the bed, watching him try to rest between vomiting spells, while the doctor asked questions, trying to decide what to do next. I was so relieved we were finally at a hospital! I knew if I just got him here, we'd be OK.

The words I heard in that moment were chilling. They made my stomach turn. The voice said, "This is it. You are about to know what is meant by *nothing lasts forever*."

The calm I had started to feel turned to fear, then overwhelming anger. Where are these thoughts coming from? Why the fuck would I think something like that right now? What is wrong with me?

I couldn't take my eyes off my favorite boy, lying in that big bed. I was surreally aware of the direction things were going, while trying so hard to change the narrative and hope for a different ending. I wanted nothing more than to be wrong.

Within a couple of hours, he would slip into a coma. A couple more hours after that, I would be told there would be nothing more they could do. How did that voice know?

I have never told anyone about the voice, until now.

Chapter 3

I Am Afraid For My Other Children

If it happened once, it can happen again.

It took 7 months to receive our autopsy results. That is a long time to wait for answers, especially when all we were given were partial answers.

We had a name for it: Porphyria. We also learned, through genetic testing, that my husband had it. Since it was a hereditary condition, we also needed to have our daughters tested.

Our second round of genetic testing took a lot of effort to make happen. There were special blood draws, arrangements outside of our hospital system with a dedicated porphyria lab, not to mention a lot begging and pleading on my part for medical professionals to participate.

Our appointment was scheduled by our pathologist at the children's hospital where my son had died. Even though everything had been set up ahead of time, there was a lot of double checking, approvals, and red tape. I desperately negotiated to convince them to just draw the blood, because the hospital system didn't have an agreement with our designated lab, they were refusing to send the samples. It was outside of their rules. However, it was the same hospital system that had done my blood draw just a few weeks earlier *and* had sent it to the same lab. I was so frustrated!

I had been instructed by our lab that these tests must be executed in a very particular way. While the pathologist had arranged for the testing to happen, I had to advocate for it to be done according to these strict standards.

Finally, they reached a decision. They would proceed with our appointment if I took ownership of both transporting and shipping the samples to our designated lab.

I took it. What else could I do?

With the day more than half over and blood samples in hand, I was sent on a quest to find a shipping company. Who knew there were so many rules about sending medical specimens? It felt like the appointment would be all for naught as I drove across town and got turned away multiple times. Then, finally, the universe took pity.

Child loss has taught me to advocate harder than I ever knew was possible. It has shown me, the hard way, that medical professionals are human, and that hospitals and doctors don't always have the answers we need.

My son's death began our journey to become experts on a rare blood disease that now impacted every member of our family. Yes, my daughters also tested positive.

This diagnosis required us to check every single medication for safety. The wrong thing in their system could set off an attack, and there are so many potential triggers! Hormone changes, diet, infection, stress... how had we made it 7 years without a single sign?!

Once again, life shifted. Not only did I yearn for answers as to why my son died from a disease we didn't know about and that shouldn't have killed him, but I became obsessed with them, because this disease coursed through my family's veins. I needed to know we would be prepared if or when it all happened again.

When you lose a child, regardless of the circumstances, you over analyze everything. If I had only done this. What if we had done that? Would it have made a difference if we knew exactly what we were dealing with? The same happens with any diagnosis.

There were some things that happened that night that I looked back on with concern. Was his first scan read correctly? Did they administer the right meds, at the right time, given the diagnoses being considered? Based on all of my research – and I did a *ton* – I still had questions. We needed to be prepared for the next time.

The next time... the fact that it was even a possibility sent chills down my spine.

I wasn't really looking for a medical error or reason to file a lawsuit, though I would have loved to have had something else to blame, someone to direct my anger towards. I just needed to know if everything had been done correctly, and if so, we still would've had the same outcome. My mental health required it.

I had asked to be in direct communication with the pathologist conducting the autopsy. We exchanged numerous emails as we searched for answers. I was directed to my pediatrician's office if I wanted someone to review the medical files and answer my questions. Unfortunately, they shut down that avenue of help, refusing to review the records, citing instructions from their legal team.

Every question seemed to be met with fear. It felt like they were all trying to hide a mistake. Their reactions forced us to adjust our strategy. We enlisted legal help.

Again, our goal wasn't to file a lawsuit.

I was desperate to have someone review the medical records and tell me we did everything right and what we should do if the same thing happens again. To even have a shot at surviving this loss, I needed my questions answered. All I met were more roadblocks.

As it happened, the people reviewing the cases have limited medical knowledge. Since there was nothing egregious, we were told there was no case. That was it. Case closed. We were once again pointed back to our pediatrician's office to get the answers we were seeking. No new information was given.

Part of accepting your child is gone is knowing, beyond a shadow of doubt, that all the right decisions were made, that there was nothing that could have been done to change the outcome. Even if that wasn't true, I needed to know what we missed. At least that would validate my guilty conscience. All we kept getting was the runaround.

So, once again, we shifted our approach and found our own medical expert.

We spent a lot of money to hire an ER doctor, outside of our local hospital affiliation, who freelances with law firms as a medical expert on malpractice cases. It took about a month, but I got my answers.

He devoured the medical records, read the scans and test results, researched, and spent an hour on the phone with us, discussing his findings. Not once did he shy away from any concern we expressed. It was exactly what I needed, to have someone tell me the truth and lay it all out on the table. He also told us Cameron's case should be published in the *New England Journal of Medicine* for others to learn from, as it was that important, but our hospital system wouldn't ever acknowledge the suggestion.

I don't believe there is closure in child loss, but that day I gained about as much closure as you can possibly achieve. Not only did he tell me what could have been done differently, he confirmed that even if those decisions had been made perfectly and medications administered at the precise moment known, it would not have been enough time to make an impact. My son had deteriorated far too quickly.

The biggest takeaway from that phone call was learning that there likely wasn't an ER in the country prepared to deal with such a condition as it had presented with Cameron that night. It would take a team of doctors with very specific expertise and access to medications that aren't readily available. So, we had work to do.

When one of your children dies, it doesn't matter what the circumstances are, you fear for your other children. If it happened once, it can happen again. Sometimes it is irrational. Even when you logically know you are overreacting, your body remembers.

The extent of those fears and the triggers are different for each of us. They may be silent and unnoticed by everyone else, but they never go away.

Porphyria changed our lives in the most dramatic way possible.

Our Diagnosis – Porphyria 101

Porphyria has come to mean a lot of things. I hold a piece of paper that tells me it is the reason my 7-year-old son died. DNA testing tells me everyone in my family has it. When I speak with doctors, there is either confusion or questions.

Most tell me they can't believe our story because, "people don't die from porphyria". Especially not 7-year-old boys with no history of symptoms. But it happened!

What I have learned: It is a blood disease. It is quite rare. According to the American Porphyria Foundation, only 2 in 1 million are "lucky enough" to claim our version of it. Most doctors have never seen a case in real life. Some remember learning about it in medical school. It makes us all nervous.

Going forward, we require a team of doctors for very basic things I've always taken for granted. I don't like feeling like the expert when I'm talking to a doctor that isn't. I can't be the one responsible for ensuring the health and safety of my girls. It terrifies me. We all know how things went the first time.

While I'm far more prepared now, I wish I had doctors that seemed more confident. Instead, it feels as if they look to me for information.

Our version of porphyria is Hereditary Coproporphyria (HCP). Ours is an acute version, meaning the symptoms are non-specific.

Due to the similarity of symptoms from other common conditions, it typically goes undiagnosed or misdiagnosed. The possibility exists to have it and not know it. It can lie dormant for years and then all of a sudden become active.

When porphyria is active, it shows itself through an attack. In our acute version, that means symptoms like severe abdominal pain, vomiting, agitation, confusion, abnormal behavior, numbness and muscle weakness, even paralysis.

What brings it on? This is not always known. However, there is a laundry list of things that we must avoid for safety precautions. Such as numerous medications, even over the counter, common items, as well as low-calorie diets, infection, stress, alcohol, even hormones, and pregnancy.

Porphyria is more commonly active in women versus men because estrogen plays a role as a trigger. What does this mean for my girls? When they reach puberty, they have a higher risk of being affected. One day, if they decide to have children, it will impact their decision and path to motherhood. They will not be able to take birth control pills, as they are considered unsafe.

Every medication they are given will need to be checked. Their pediatrician and even their dentist must make sure every decision is made in their best interest. It is our hope that symptoms remain dormant for our youngest. She only has one kidney, and porphyria attacks cause damage to kidneys.

When one of my girls is sick, I am triggered and rendered incompetent through fear.

How am I supposed to know the difference between regular sick and porphyria sick? According to Cameron's autopsy report, his brain showed signs of previous attacks. That baffles me. Nothing stands out as anything more than normal illness. We missed it then. Why not now? Or in the future?

I can assure you our pediatrician now knows me! She gave me her personal cell phone number so I can reach her anytime. I wish that made me feel all warm and fuzzy inside. It doesn't.

There is only one person recognized as a porphyria expert in the state of Florida. She is based in Miami. I have spoken with her on a few occasions. We are still searching for local doctors to be part of our "team" so we can have all of our bases covered.

This diagnosis sits in the background of everything we do, just waiting. Those two little girls resemble a ticking time bomb, sitting in the palm of my hand. All I can do is try to be rational each time they get sick. With time and knowledge, it will hopefully get easier.

I know that is just wishful thinking.

Chapter 4

I Killed My Son

I knew better, but I went against my gut and administered the medication that unleashed my son's porphyria attack. If you were to ask my husband, he would tell you it was his fault, because he bought it.

Regardless, we both feel tremendous guilt. At the same time, there is no one to blame, so guilt is misplaced.

Two weeks before my son died, he had developed a cold. It was bad enough that I took him to the minute clinic to be seen. He was really congested with a sore throat and cough. Overall, he felt terrible, and I wanted to rule out infection.

The doctor wrote him a prescription, an antibiotic for his ears. She also recommendation purchasing Afrin, or any over-the-counter nasal spray. She said he was at the age where it was safe to use and it would help him breathe easier, which would help him feel better.

As I waited for his prescription to be filled, I walked the aisles of the drugstore, looking for the things that would bring him symptom relief. As I knelt to examine the nasal spray options, I had a really odd feeling come over me. I just *knew* I shouldn't buy it, that he shouldn't take it.

That feeling stood out to me in a way I still cannot describe, a way that made me pause. I used nasal spray every time I had a cold. So, why would I hesitate in allowing my son, who was now at a "safe" age, to also take it?

As I stood with the bottle in my hand, I couldn't shake the overwhelming feeling he shouldn't have it. It was like that voice I had heard. As weird as it sounds, I put the bottle back and decided he would just need to suffer through his congestion.

Fast forward 2 weeks, my husband stood in that same aisle with the same bottle in his hand. The cold was back. Another doctor was now making the same recommendation. This time, my husband, who has never used nasal spray, decided to purchase it.

When he unloaded the bag on my kitchen counter, I felt it again. Something pressed me to listen.

I told my husband about my crazy premonition from 2 weeks prior. He was now used to me starting sentences with the phrase, "This is going to sound crazy, but…".

As I shared my strange gut feeling, we debated. Give it to him? Don't give it to him?

Our decision was obvious. I couldn't come up with a logical reason why I would have such a guttural response to it. Now, I know.

That night, Christmas Eve, around 7 o'clock, I began the process of administering the nasal spray. I called Cameron to the kitchen table. While I sat in a chair, he stood in front of me. I explained what the medication was, that I used it, and how it would help him breathe a little easier while he was sick.

I demonstrated that we would insert it into his nose, plug the other side, squeeze, and he would sniff.

The feeling that I should stop was so overwhelming, nagging me, but I shoved it aside and proceeded.

No medical professional would ever confirm our suspicions. That night, when we had arrived at the hospital, I asked the doctor about nasal spray. It was the only thing that was different about any other time he had been sick; but it was dismissed, because how could it be related?! Surely the medication wasn't tainted.

We brought it up again with the pathologist. She told us there was no way of knowing, again focusing on the idea it would be tainted, he would have had different toxins in his system.

When we had our diagnosis, my husband scoured the internet, looking for any connection to a living porphyria patient and the active ingredient oxymetazoline. At the time, he had *one* hit. I wish we had printed the page, because no sooner did he find it, their website changed, and it was gone.

Medications are listed and noted for safety in a database on the American Porphyria Foundation[4] website. Each drug is classified in one of five ways: OK!, OK?, BAD?, BAD!, and NO INFO. When we looked up oxymetazoline, it was listed as "OK?". The database referenced one study stating it is

---

[4] American Porphyria Foundation. (2010-2022). *Drug Safety Database Search* [online]. Available at: https://porphyriafoundation.org/drugdatabase/drug-safety-database-search/ [Accessed May 11, 2022]

"probably not porphyrinogenic", and a second study stating it is "unsafe for patients".

This drug being a key catalyst in Cameron's death was the only thing that made sense to us.

Years later, we found another instance online that referenced[5] oxymetazoline hydrochloride nasal solution, stating it has been associated with acute attacks of porphyria and is considered unsafe in porphyric patients.

Had we only known. Had I only listened to my gut.

We may not have directly or intentionally killed our son, but the guilt still feels the same.

---

[5] Drugster.org. (2019). *Drugster Encyclopedia* [online]. Available at: https://www.drugfuture.com/mt/oxymetazoline-hydrochloride.pdf [Accessed May 11, 2022]

Chapter 5

How Do I Survive This?

We are not taught how to lose things. Therefore, when we experience death, we find ourselves in unfamiliar territory. The death of a child sends us reeling. Children aren't supposed to die! It's not the natural order of things. It isn't fair!

Yet, here we stand, smack dab in the middle of the unfair. A place we never expected to be, and one we certainly weren't prepared for. We need a new word for it. Unfair is nowhere near harsh enough a description.

Navigating the loss of a child is overwhelming. We shouldn't have to do this! We don't want to do this. We don't have a choice.

What do we do now? That's a question I have asked myself over and over.

There is no rule book, no map. We must rely on what we are taught about grief. Unfortunately, those lessons are lacking. The things we are conditioned to believe about grief are wrong.

As a child, we are taught to believe anger, frustration, and sadness are bad behaviors. If we threw a tantrum or showed any semblance of unhappiness, we were corrected or punished. The message was consistent, this wasn't how you behaved.

When these feelings invade and take over, and boy do they ever, there is an immediate gut reaction to suppress them, to hide them, to let them make you feel like you are doing something wrong.

This includes crying. As a child, the moment tears began to fall, you were likely hushed and whisked away from everyone else.

Any display of emotion causes discomfort to those around you. Therefore, you learn at a young age to mask these feelings, hide your "negative" emotions, and cry in private.

Don't give in to those lies and false expectations of what grief should look like. All of those emotions and reactions are healthy, appropriate, and expected. Feel them all. Allow them proper space. The important thing is to do so in a safe way.

I found the conditioning didn't stop there.

No one talked about death! When it happened, the conversation was brief. "How sad for the family. They were such a great person." The end.

The polite thing to do was send a sympathy card, have flowers delivered to the funeral home, and, assuming that you knew them well enough, attend the memorial service. You would say, "I'm so sorry for your loss." Give a hug. Life moved on.

I thought I had a lot of experience with death before my son died. I had lived through the loss of 4 great-grandparents. I felt the loss of a cousin. My immediate family had stories of babies and young children no longer with us, though they weren't often spoken. Several classmates from school had died young. No one I was personally close to, but I grew up in a small town, so I knew of them.

Each loss was different; but my impression of it was the same.

We were sad for their families, as well as ourselves. We gave cards, flowers, and hugs. We contemplated the meaning of life, how short it was and that we should make the most of every moment. Then, it appeared that life moved on. Everyone went back to the way they were before.

What I realize now is that life didn't move on for everyone. Things never go back to the way they were before.

I knew nothing about death or grief.

I was 8 years old when I had my first experience with death. When Gram died, I remember feeling confused. I knew what death was, yet, it was the first time it had impacted my immediate family. Weeks after her death, I remember crying at night, alone. I was so shocked she was gone, and I was never given the chance to say goodbye. It felt incomplete.

Then, there was the guilt. Why, as an 8-year-old child, would I feel guilt over my great-grandmother's death? I didn't cry at the funeral home. My mother took us to the viewing, but all I could do was try to make jokes to lighten the mood. I couldn't cry like everyone else around me. Emotions made me uncomfortable! I felt like there was something wrong with me, like I was doing it all wrong.

What struck me, even at that age, was that people stopped talking about her death after the funeral. My guess is the adults talked about it, but not when us kids were around. I was given the false impression that everyone had just moved on, that they were OK.

This experience molded each future encounter I would have with death. I should show sadness, but for only a short time. I should cry alone. I should move on, though secretly harbor feelings of unresolved grief.

As I got older, I would watch people who had experienced profound loss. Quietly studying them, I would often wonder how they continued to live. How their world wasn't blown apart. I was always in awe of their perceived ability to move on with their lives. I also wondered what remained hidden from our eyes.

When my son died, my eyes were opened to grief – wide open! The reality of loss, what it was like to have your world turned upside down by death, to have everything blown apart and NOT be able to just move on. I was drowning in it.

Nothing had prepared me, nor could it, for the wreckage and chaos that would remain for years – *years!* In a way, it had taken up residence. It was here to stay.

We were overwhelmed by the outpouring of "I'm sorry", the sending of flowers, and the attendance at my son's memorial. We learned quickly how to put on a brave face and mask the unbearable pain, how to become the people I used to watch and analyze.

Most of all, we learned that no one seemed to understand.

"At least you still have your girls..."

"He is in a much better place..."

"Remember, he is always with you in your heart..."

"Stay strong, in time it will get better..."

"I don't know how you are still standing, I could never..."

It became very apparent to me the words we are conditioned to speak, the sentiments we always believed about loss, were wrong!

Everyone had advice. Yet, none of it was good. They all wanted to fix us, to help us get back to the person we were before. We never go back to who we were. It is impossible.

Very few people knew what we were going through. We were living every parent's worst nightmare, and we had no idea what we were doing.

Survival mode is a scary place to exist.

You question everything. Where did my son go? Is there something after this life? Is he OK? Could I have done anything different? What am I supposed to do now? Does this ever get easier?

The emotions of sadness, shock, frustration, anger, and pure hatred take over. Life feels so heavy and exhausting. You can't move. The idea of living without your child is torture. You start to feel crazy because the things you think and experience are unlike anything you could have imagined. You compare your grief to that of others, or what others had told you it should be. No one gets it.

You feel so alone!

Everyone attempts words of comfort, but it all begins to feel like judgement. You aren't doing things right. You shouldn't act that way. You are wrong for feeling this way. You should be further along in your grief journey. Just forgive. You need to find a way to move on.

What people don't understand is this loss extends beyond just the physical loss of our child. There is not a single aspect of our life untouched by it… by grief.

People scatter and retreat. Friends don't know what to say, so they shrink away and choose silence. Family creates pressure, both real and perceived. Some of the people you thought would be there to pick you up in your lowest possible moments seem to disappear.

Your hopes and dreams for the future, a life with your child, is ripped away. Not only that, but your entire daily routine is changed. There is no lunch to pack, homework to argue over, laundry to wash, or messes to clean up. You have an empty seat at the table and in your car. The house can be so noisy and yet all you hear is the deafening silence.

If you have other children, you never parent the same way. It's a fine line to walk between modeling healthy grief and destroying your living children's self-worth. My oldest daughter asked us if we would be this sad if she had been the one to die. Everything is broken.

When you look in the mirror, you don't even recognize your own reflection staring back at you! You pray for death, even if you are not suicidal, even if you no longer believe in any god. Death would be perfect. A piece of you already died with them anyway.

This kind of grief can take you to really dark places.

Child loss is a significant trauma. For me, it was 9 months before his death stopped playing over and over on a movie reel inside my head. It was longer than that for my PTSD triggers to subside.

Most people don't realize you can get PTSD after your child dies. They only attribute it to those who have gone through war, but I assure you... we have.

When nighttime came, I found myself paralyzed by a fear I had never felt before. I couldn't enter our kitchen area, especially when the lights were low. My heart would race, anxiety raged, and I would be overcome with a crushing physical fear. Even though I could rationalize it, I had no control.

My oldest daughter was 4 years old and the baby only 6 months when my son died. They had to sleep in my room at night or I never would have been able to walk across the house at night if they cried out.

There was something about that combination of the sun going down and being in my kitchen area, the room where we tended my son before his death, that would trigger a massive panic attack. I've never felt so terrified.

Before bed, I would gather every single item I could possibly need during the night and store it in my bedroom. Anything I forgot was impossible to retrieve.

In those days, surviving just happened. I wasn't trying… I didn't know how to do that anymore; nor did I even care. It took too much effort, and my energy was depleted.

People were quick to offer their suggestions, even when I hadn't asked for them, especially those who had no clue what they were talking about.

I found myself smiling and nodding, like being polite and not causing any friction was socially dictated.

Inside, I raged. How dare they try to tell me what I should or shouldn't do. What the fuck do they know? I used that word a lot. No words in existence were powerful enough to match the hatred I felt inside. Language simply failed to do it justice.

People tried so hard to fix me. I didn't want to be fixed. Our society is conditioned to believe happiness is the only acceptable state of being. Grief is bad. Except, it's not. I wanted to grieve. I wanted to feel pain. In fact, I didn't think I felt enough pain!

While the outside world agonized over what they thought I was going through, I knew their external view didn't even scratch the surface of my reality. I had no interest in finding a solution that would make me feel better.

I raged even more because very few people were willing to just accept my ugliness... sit in the middle of it all and just be. Instead, they made unvalidated assumptions about my grief and they all pointed to a need for it to end.

Surviving the death of our children is something that just happens. We are the only ones who get to decide the quality and condition of that survival.

It took me a long time to realize *I* was the only one who knew what would work for *me*. I was the only one who knew what was right or wrong. I was also the only one who could decide if or when it was time for my grief to lessen; but I knew it would never end!

It's difficult to break the patterns of behavior you have held your entire life, to stop living according to someone else's expectation, to undo the need to follow the rules and to constantly pursue a state of happiness. It was hard to stop caring what anyone else thought or felt.

In a way, grief has made me selfish. I couldn't be concerned with how others were doing or try to make them feel better. I would often hear, "You're not the only one grieving," or "We lost him, too." I get that, but my loss is different. I am his mother. He was mine.

I see this selfishness as a good thing. The only way to heal and survive this loss is to place ourselves and our needs first. It can ruffle some feathers, though.

Even as time goes on, our actions can be questioned. We've kept their things for too long. We talk about them too much. We still celebrate their birthday. We still cry or grieve years later. These actions defy what everyone has been conditioned to believe about grief. So, it can't possibly be healthy... right?!

Wrong!

What people don't understand is that no matter what you see on social media or in public, even if it appears everything is fine, underneath it all, bereaved parents are still grieving. How could they not? Their child is gone. They will always grieve that loss. Time heals nothing!

It was hard to put myself first.

It also saved my sanity.

The Advice I Wish I Got When My Son Died

When my son died, I received a lot of advice. I found people do not know what to say. They default to the things they have been conditioned to say during these times. It came from many different sources, most of which had never lost a child. The advice came from good intentions, but it was hollow, not at all what I needed in that moment.

When someone would tell me it would be OK, I was angry. They would say everything happens for a reason and I should trust God. More anger. Then, there was the, "Give it time. Time heals all wounds." It doesn't. There were the people who tried to facilitate a connection, "Here, call Jane. She lost her son, too." I was not in a place to talk to other bereaved mothers and hear all about their experience. Everything felt like pressure towards a direction someone else thought was best for me. Someone who had never stood where I was standing.

If you haven't noticed, there is a lot of anger in grief. It is unavoidable, so you should just learn to embrace it early. It made me feel like I was going crazy. Everything made me mad. I hated their advice, yet I found myself starting to wonder if I should listen. It didn't resonate, but I was desperate. So, I started judging my grief. It made me question everything I was doing and feel as if I was doing it all wrong. That made me more angry.

Then, I had a breakthrough – a grief breakthrough.

I don't recall the cause or the source, but I suddenly understood what I needed to do. It all made sense.

My epiphany was this: My grief is only about me. The journey I walk is my own. No one can tell me how to do it. I simply have to do whatever I feel is right in the moment for me.

It is not my job to help make others feel better. I cannot be concerned about how they are doing. I know it sounds harsh and unfeeling; however, there is an "I" in grief. As there should be. And it's right smack dab in the middle. That tells me that I am at the center of my own grief journey. It is the only way because *my* son died! This was about Cameron and me; no one else. The rest of the world has their own path to follow, and they must figure it out on their own.

It seemed so simple. It felt selfish, but simple.

Since my son died, I have changed the way I talk to anyone who has experienced loss. I never tell them I am sorry. I hated hearing that phrase. I am no longer afraid to say, "That really sucks!" It does. Then, I tell them I am thinking about them and sending love. I really am. Love is all that matters.

If I feel the urge to share advice, I simply tell them their grief is unique to them. They have to do whatever is right for them and not compare themselves to anyone else. Don't worry about what anyone else tells you. Just follow your gut.

This advice would have saved me so much agony.

…..

There is a difference between caring about everyone else and becoming their caregiver through this experience. I couldn't take that on. I didn't have the energy or the interest. I could only take care of me.

Once I began to adopt that mindset, things did begin to shift for me. I started to recognize all the ways I gave other people control and let them get into my head.

I realized when I was making decisions that were best for me, survival felt a little bit easier.

Chapter 6

Welcome To The Worst Club Ever

My life rapidly unraveled around me. I felt helpless. The false sense of security that had plagued my entire life was shattered and I could now see with plain sight. We have zero control over anything. ZERO! Best intentions, well-laid plans, prayers, so-called experts… none of it made an ounce of difference.

My 7-year-old son. My first-born, only son, died… on Christmas… on my birthday.

He went from healthy to "beyond repair" in 12 hours. My entire world spiraled and went dark.

In motherhood, we joke about "keeping the kids alive" on particularly challenging days. We may not have been perfect, but at least we kept the kids alive. Cheers to that! Apparently, keeping them alive is considered doing the bare minimum to get by.

Those jokes used to make me chuckle. Now, I hate them.

I'm the mom that couldn't keep my kid alive!

We did everything right that night, given the information we had to work with. Except, I failed. My kid died.

I must not have fought hard enough, pleaded hard enough, prayed hard enough. I wasn't religious, so God just didn't care. In the big picture of the universe, we didn't matter.

What did we do to deserve this ending? I felt guilty, jaded, angry, hatred, and out of control!

Life could pretty much suck it. Whatever god people prayed to, I gave a big middle finger. Where was the miracle I so desperately needed? Why wasn't my son "good enough" to be saved?

That night, as the Chaplain quietly lurked in the hallway and made her attempt to sit with us in support, my mind screamed, "Take your god and shove it." This was just the start of my anger.

The amount of hate that surged through my veins is hard to describe.

The days became a blur. A dense fog rolled in and covered everything in a heavy layer of grief. My mind became hazy and scattered. It was hard to breathe. I felt like I was drowning.

Mentally, emotionally, and physically exhausted, I wanted to curl up and die. I didn't eat. I cried. My mind was consumed by the gaping hole that was left when my son was ripped away. It was all I saw.

I was thrust into a life I didn't want. A life I didn't choose, one I absolutely hated. Do you know how hard it is to imagine living the rest of your life tortured in this way?

If you've lost a child, I know you do!

You feel so alone, even standing in a room full of family and friends. There is no one who can begin to understand the depths of your pain; but I assure you, you are not alone. I understand.

The moment your child died, you gained entry to this club: Child Loss Club. I thought it only existed for other people. I didn't want in, but membership isn't a choice.

I didn't know it at the time, but this club would become my refuge, my people. It still seems crazy to me that this group of strangers is where I would feel most seen and comforted.

At the time though, I didn't want it.

As I reflected on my life and my preoccupation with watching bereaved mothers, I wondered if the reason I was here was because I unconsciously made it happen. Some weird form of karma or self-fulfilling prophecy. Either way, I felt punished.

Early on, everyone wanted me to talk to someone they knew who had lost a child. If I could just hear from someone else, it would help pull me out of my funk. The problem was, I didn't want to hear their stories of hope. The idea of someone telling me I would get through this, that I would be OK, made me physically sick. I didn't want any of this.

Now, I'm the person everyone is told to talk to.

People reach out to me often and ask if I will talk to someone they know who just lost a child. Like my speech is the one that can rally them and fix their grief, because that's what they really want as they orchestrate these conversations. They want to fix us, or have others be fixed and feel better.

Child loss isn't something you fix, however, which is why I always politely decline these requests. While I am happy to talk to anyone about their loss, they need to want that discussion themselves. For me, it was a long time before I cared what anyone else's experience was. I only cared about my own and how devastated I was. I like to remind people it's OK to be in that state.

Grief is unique and abides by no timeline. We must be our own keepers. As our lives become unrecognizable, only we can decide when it's time to look for help or seek a way back. Though we never really go back to who we were. We are forever changed.

Who am I to tell another bereaved parent they can do this? Who am I to decide that's even the message they want or need to hear?

Sometimes we just want to *not* be OK. And that, in itself, is OK.

Sometimes we wish we could take a baseball bat to our entire lives and destroy every single thing that even hints at goodness, because it has no place here.

Sometimes we fantasize about cutting ties, walking away... just leaving everything and everyone because this life feels unbearable.

And then there are times we wish we could just die, too.

These are incredibly scary things for our friends and family to comprehend. It places them in a state of pure helplessness and discomfort. I honestly believe you can't understand it until you experience it. While we want to be understood, we don't want them to understand this.

There are unspoken expectations and unexpected heartbreak. We know it's hard to live, but it's also hard to watch.

People disappear. Even those people who you thought would be there at the lowest possible moments of your life. They can't handle the darkness that has become your life.

It's hard to be in this club. There is so much pressure, both real and self-inflicted. Everyone wants us to feel better... to not be so sad... to find a way through... to survive.

Sometimes we just want it all to go away.

Forever has new meaning: torture.

How do we keep going? I can't imagine my life without him!

Life is so unfair. I realized that statement never held meaning until that moment. I didn't want to do this! I hated this! The anger and despair were overwhelming, and the situation felt impossible.

I constantly told myself to not focus too long on the idea that it's over. If you allow yourself to stay there very long, it will crush your soul and pull the breath from your lungs.

Please know you are not alone, though it will feel that way.

It sucks being a member of this club. None of us ever expected to join. While every parent thinks about what it may feel like to lose a child, no one ever believes it can really happen. Unfortunately, it does.

It happened to me.

Chapter 7

Does It Get Easier?

A lot of people told me to, "Hang in there, give it time."

I didn't want things to get better. In fact, I wanted it to be worse. The destruction of my life felt invisible. I wanted to physically feel the pain I felt emotionally. I fantasized about all the ways I could ruin my life… an affair, driving my car full speed into a brick wall, cutting my arm just to feel it bleed, just disappearing without a trace and never coming back.

Frustrated, I knew there wasn't a solution that would match the suffering I would want to feel. So, I did nothing.

You do a lot of nothing in grief… for a *long* time.

In my world, loss didn't come with a sudden revelation of deep appreciation and love for what I had left. I didn't suddenly look at my girls and feel an extra outpouring of emotion. There were no happy reunions with people from my past or an overwhelming feeling to forgive past transgressions.

I felt nothing.

It would be a year before I knew my husband felt the same way. Just one of the things we kept hidden in shame. I guess a part of me didn't have the guts to blow my own world apart, and I was sure confessing my real thoughts would be the lighter fluid to my flame.

The funny thing about grief like this is you both wish for the pain to end and fear the day it stops hurting. I didn't want time to make it easier. My heart told me easier meant I was "getting over it".

I vowed to never get over my son's death.

He made me a mother. He was my world. I couldn't imagine my life without him, though I was now living it... or at least existing in it. A piece of me died that day. If this loss ever felt easier, it had to mean I was forgetting him. That was impossible to do!

I refused.

My path began to cross with other bereaved parents. They would reach out for advice, believing I had everything figured out, because I was sharing our story publicly. The question I always got was, "Does it ever get easier?"

This is a tricky question to answer.

I lived in a complete grief fog for 9 months. My husband and I found ourselves slumped side-by-side on the couch, just existing. Days were unproductive. They ran together. We still had our two young daughters to care for. To say it was hard is an understatement.

It felt damn near impossible to care for my own basic needs. Still, I was responsible for two little girls' lives... something I did not believe I should be in charge of.

I will never forget the PTSD, though I am positive a little bit will always follow me.

It surprised me. The sheer terror I felt at night, it took my breath away. That fear gripped my heart and completely paralyzed me.

I avoided his corner of the house, even during the day… his bedroom, the bathroom, his little hallway. Even years later, I still feel a tinge of anxiety that I believe will never completely fade.

Trauma changes us. That's what child loss is, it's trauma. Though, it took me a really long time to recognize it as such.

Just like in childbirth, you never get a manual to tell you what to expect and shine a light on your path.

People think the first year of loss is the hardest. All the milestones, the firsts. It's not true. Year one was hard, but it may surprise you to hear many bereaved parents will tell you year two is harder.

Brace yourself!

It becomes abundantly clear just how much the rest of the world has moved on.

Here you are, still barely treading water, seemingly alone. Friends become strangers. Strangers become friends.

My son's death has damaged my relationship with family. In some instances, these were things I deemed unforgiveable. In other instances, I just couldn't handle the grief triggers I felt simply being near them. So, I placed distance to protect my own heart.

Actions are misunderstood. Feelings are hurt. Everyone is grieving. Child loss is a minefield. No one knows what to do, what to say. Not doing or saying anything can be even more hurtful. It is a no-win situation for anyone.

On the positive side, you quickly learn who your friends are. Who has your back. Those select few people who roll up their sleeves and climb into the trenches with you, seek to understand. They are everything! If you have those people, consider yourself lucky.

Life takes on new meaning. We realize we wasted so much time on things that simply don't matter. The important things become crystal clear. The rest? Who cares!

There is no going back to the person we were before. We can't. We wouldn't want to, even if that person still existed.

This grief journey is lonely! We miss the person we were before, the life we had before. We intensely miss it! We no longer recognize who we are or know what we need.

No matter how much we want it, there is no going back.

Does it ever get easier? My answer is always yes and no.

The keyword there is *and*. You will find it punctuates every aspect of your life now. Everything becomes a dichotomy. All our happiness now comes with sadness. We are living and a part of us is dead. Grief causes us to move forward and take steps back.

If we are honest about where we stand, we realize losing a child is never easy. There are always milestones, long after you even believe it's possible. Things you never thought you would consider momentous.

Triggers are everywhere. Even if you work to manage them, you don't always know when or where they will pop up, or even what they will be. I'm told, even decades later, they can bring you to your knees. I believe them.

So, why do we not talk about it? Why can we not be honest about the realities of child loss? Are we so conditioned to wear our mask that we trick ourselves into believing we have it mastered?

I believe healing from a loss like this is a lifelong process. It's a daily practice. We must learn to recognize the triggers, understand the symptoms, feel every emotion, and learn how to maneuver through the minefield that is grief. The most challenging is that it changes over time. So, we must constantly adjust our course.

I don't think we ever really reach a point where it becomes easier, only different.

Easier is an illusion. You just get used to the weight of carrying your grief around with you. As you get better at leaning into it, allowing it, your ability to carry it improves. You can breathe easier when it shows up.

I wish more people had told me the truth about their grief.

Chapter 8

You Are So Strong

There is a quote, often shared, that says, "The bereaved mother[6]. She has experienced the unimaginable and yet she is still able to walk." When I see it, I question the definition of strength.

There is this notion that because we can get out of bed every day, we are strong. The ability to do the necessities life has demanded means we are living. People look on with amazement and say, "Wow, I don't know how you do it. There is no way I could do that!"

We are neither strong, nor are we living. If you only knew the truth.

When people would say those things to me, my mind heard things like, "You aren't doing it right," or "You didn't love your son as much as I love my child, because my world would be devastated." I know that wasn't the intent; but early on, I was unable to process any compliment related to strength. To me, grief and strength did not go hand-in-hand.

Even on day one, I got out of bed. Necessity, habit, and responsibility motivated me to put my feet on the floor and walk one foot in front of the other. Do you know what I thought

---

[6] Carly Marie Dudley. The Bereaved Mother Meme. Carlymarieprojectheal.com. Accessed at: https://www.pinterest.com.au/pin/145241156709542042/

about? I thought about the numerous times I told Cameron, "Life is full of things you don't necessarily WANT to do, but you HAVE to do them."

My words came back to haunt me. Talk about things you don't want to do!

Responsibility, not strength, took over.

On the inside, my mind was throwing an all-out tantrum and screaming to stop. It raged. Each day, I carried the weight of Cameron on my shoulders. When I moved, I could feel myself being pulled down. It was exhausting! I had no strength. Endurance barely kicked in, allowing me to do the bare minimum of tasks. It was *hard*.

Child loss is a shit storm of one thing after another. As if the death of my child wasn't enough, there seemed to be a string of constant hardships and reminders that followed; not that I could or would forget.

Some of these losses I expected, but not that that made it any easier.

Our future, or the idea of what that future would look like, was erased. Things he should have been guaranteed, things like the second grade, an eighth birthday, sleepovers with friends, learning to drive, high school graduation, and college, all faded to black. He would never feel the butterflies of falling in love for the first time. There would be no family of his own.

Then came the things I didn't think about, until they slapped me in the face.

On April 15th, we were asked how many tax deductions we are claiming. At the grocery store, a sweet old lady asked, "Are these your only two children?" A boy mom would innocently say, "Be glad you only have girls." The voicemail from the dentist's office would remind me it was time to schedule his next visit.

It took me 6 months to tell our health insurance company our son had died. We were overpaying hundreds of dollars on our premium, but that was so much easier than having to explain to the person on the other end of the phone that our 7-year-old son died, as well as having to hear the discomfort in their voice as they said, "I'm so sorry for your loss."

At least once a month, my son would get mail or an email would arrive in my inbox. The first year, it was the *Highlights* magazine subscription he would have received that year for Christmas. Now, even years later, it is a past healthcare provider's mailing list or appointment reminder cards. Not once have I picked up the phone to make it stop. It is a conversation I avoid. The mail serves as a happy reminder he existed… and a sad reminder he is gone, all at the same time.

My daughters lost a brother, their biggest fan and supporter. They will likely never remember the sound of his laughter as they giggled together. Memories of him will fade. My youngest was only 6 months old. She only knows her brother from photos and stories.

Their childhood innocence was lost with his death. They now know we can't protect them from everything. Death is not an abstract concept seen only in the movies. We will always be learning how to navigate the pain that will haunt them for the rest of their lives. As they grow older, they will see other girls with their brothers and realize what they have missed out on. As they have their own children, they will know what it means to have lost a piece of their past and their future.

My sense of security has been shattered. I know how fragile life is.

The picture of what I thought motherhood would look like was ripped from the pages of my reality. The activities I once treasured became painful, sometimes so much so I could no longer take part. The ways in which I interacted with my children shifted. My deep, profound love for them will never change, though I sometimes feel disconnected, because it looks nothing like how I envisioned it would be. How it used to be. Every experience is tainted by what's missing.

Then, there is the fear of forgetting. I fear I will forget things about him, the sound of his voice, the feeling of what it was like to share space in the same room; each memory, from the daily mundane to the most significant. I feel everyone around me is forgetting him. He is rarely a part of normal, easy conversation.

I lost a piece of myself the day my son died. My outlook on life changed. It was as if all my emotions had gone numb. I withdrew from many aspects of my former life, disengaged from relationships, and made decisions very differently than I did before.

Relationships have been desecrated or become non-existent. I was betrayed in the alteration of our words and an incorrect cause of death being published in my son's obituary. I have been told more than once to "get over it" as I wasn't the only one grieving. Friends have avoided acknowledging that anything happened. I've watched people I know do everything in their power to avoid me in public.

My circle of people shifted dramatically. For a long time, I didn't have the energy to invest in any of my relationships. I found I just didn't care about anything the way I once did. Grief like this makes us bad friends, daughters, sisters, and wives. Oftentimes, the way we survive is to withdraw.

I had to release the guilt around not keeping up with all the things society dictates are important or normal. There is nothing normal about life after child loss. Things never return to the way they were. Knowing that and accepting it are two very different things.

Conversations are now anxiety ridden, especially small talk with strangers. I must anticipate the questions they will ask, and more importantly, how I will choose to respond. Simple things like, "How many kids do you have?"

I want to answer it matter-of-factly, the same way I would have answered the question before, because it is now a fact of my life; but it's not a piece of information someone can receive in the way I want them to… the way it used to be received.

People no longer see me as a mother of three. To the outside world, I have 2 girls. The number of people that look at me and still see him is dwindling. With each new person I meet, I must decide how and when to share my story, as it can change everything.

Regardless of how I present it, sad or not, the course of the conversation swiftly changes, awkwardness enters. I can feel them physically pull back in discomfort. I hear their internal sigh of relief that it happened to someone else.

You are no longer just another mother, you become a subject to study, the stuff of nightmares. You often feel people unconsciously pull back, just in case it is something they can catch.

They all wonder at one thing: *How do you do it?* Because they never could.

Chapter 9

Grief Is Ugly

Life is no longer normal. We yearn for the normal we once knew, but it's not possible to return there. Even if you could figure out how to go back to the way things were, it would never be the same. We wouldn't want it to be the same. How could it be? There is a huge piece missing. If things ever went back to the way they were, it would be like saying it didn't matter that my child is no longer here. *It matters!*

Let's be honest. The new normal sucks! Even when you find joy again, there is a piece of you that knows your joy is different. People may not see it, but the person you once were is gone!

Sometimes, I feel disconnected from the rest of the world. Even though others around me can't necessarily see it, child loss sets me apart. Grief adds an intangible complexity to life. The way I think about things and see the world is through the lens of loss.

I sometimes struggle to connect with people. The conversations I used to have don't fulfill me in the same way. I am constantly assessing how much to share, who to share it with, and gauge how much it will freak them out. Most times, it is easier to not engage.

If you are lucky, you have at least one person in your life that wades into your mess and refuses to leave. I am thankful to have more than one.

Yet, there are often dark things that are hard to share with those outside of this club.

I think horrible thoughts. I feel such shame, though I know it is just my grief.

Like that time in the drive thru of a fast-food restaurant. Our wait was extended for unknown reasons. As we arrived at the window, the cashier apologized, stating there had been an emergency in the restaurant, as a small child had started choking, and they had to call 911. She quickly added, "But don't worry. Everyone is OK." Do you know my next thought? It was not a sigh of relief or happiness for that family (though I'm glad for their outcome). Instead, my mind went to, "Sure they are, because that's how it works for other people; but not for us."

Then, there is the parent posting on social media about their child's birthday. They lament because another year has passed, and their child is getting older. I fight the urge to comment, "At least your kid is still alive." But I won't use "at least" because I know how crappy that phrase is.

I hold a ticking time bomb, destined to destroy every future conversation I have. My husband and I "joke" about all the ways we could drop the phrase "Yeah, well, my son died" into those conversations where people are trying to one up you on how bad things are. This joking is our only outlet to find a way to laugh about it so it doesn't feel so horrible.

Sometimes, I want so badly to drop this bomb as a way to shift perspective. Motherhood is hard! I will never fault someone for venting their frustrations or sharing their stories. However, I find an insane number of instances where I want to drop the "At least your kid didn't die" bomb, allowing it to slap people back into reality and make them realize what they are complaining about is insignificant.

Don't complain to me about trivial things like they are the end of the world. They are not! Things *could* be far worse. Let me tell you how… but I don't.

Everyday conversations can feel like a minefield. Even completely innocent comments made in your vicinity can feel like a dagger to your heart.

Like the first time I visited home, the summer after my son died. He was the first boy grandchild. People would always comment about him being the only boy. That summer, I listened as everyone commented about my nephew being the only boy among all these girls. It was like my son had never existed and had been replaced. I know it wasn't their intention, but it hurt. These moments happen all the time.

I can see people walk on eggshells around me. They are afraid everything they say will cause me pain or make me remember. I'm here to tell you, I have not forgotten. There isn't a single thing you could say that would suddenly make me remember. It is always there. While there is a good chance you could say something that would make me cringe, saying nothing or avoiding the topic altogether feels far more offensive.

It really is a no-win situation. So, I appreciate the people willing to exist in the discomfort, ask questions, and bring up the topics that everyone else tries to ignore.

It doesn't matter how much time has gone by. I will always see the space my son should fill. I will always wonder how things would be different if he was still here. I will love hearing his name!

Even years later, I still watch mothers with their sons and feel jealousy. I had that once, but now it's gone. Even if they know how lucky they are, they don't really. It is impossible for them to imagine where I stand and how it really impacts my life.

Honestly, there is a piece of me that hates them. It's not so much them, per se, but that I am now forced to watch them interact in the ways I want to, but can't. Life's cruel way of twisting the knife a little bit, reminding me once again of what I lost.

I don't need reminders. Though, they are everywhere. Every day I feel his absence.

This causes us to withdraw a bit (actually, *a lot*). It's a coping mechanism, a safety net to protect our hearts, even in the slightest.

I wouldn't want them to know that reality. Yet, I can't help but feel pain.

Dear Boy Moms: I Don't Really Hate You, But I Do[7]

You probably don't notice, but I watch you from the corner of my eye. A mix of anger, jealousy, despair, and yearning bubbles under the surface.

When our eyes happen to meet, I smile. I'm sure you think I am merely admiring your little boy as I pass by.

But there's more going on...

You see, I used to be you, before my son died. When I look at any mother and son together, my grief triggers. You have exactly what I want. Regardless of how messy, chaotic, or exhausting it may be at this exact moment, I wish I were you.

Behind your eyes, I see a familiar look. One death stole from me. It is a look one unknowingly has when life is as it should be.

Seeing you interact, doing routine things I once took for granted, feels like a stab to my heart. It makes the ugly side of grief come out. The stuff I try hard to keep hidden because the world wouldn't understand.

The thing that, if you knew, would make me look bad.

The ugly side of grief never goes away. It makes me hate you.

I don't hate you, but more your perfectly imperfect life. What I see in you reminds me of how much I've lost, how much I hate my new normal without my son.

---

[7] Graham, E. (2018). *Dear Boy Moms: I Don't Hate You, But I Do*. Still Standing Magazine. https://stillstandingmag.com/2018/06/17/dear-boy-moms/

Sometimes it's hard to separate the two.

It can feel like there is a wall between us. There is. I appear to remain distant and disengaged. This is just one of my coping mechanisms. Getting too close makes me vulnerable to the pain I try so hard to keep locked up.

Internally, I'm screaming, "That should be me!"

It should be. It's not natural living without my son. Knowing a part of me, one that should still be here, isn't. The trauma of that loss extends into aspects of my life I never thought possible. It's something I continuously work to manage.

When I innocently see the two of you, it can cause the walls I've built around my heart to shift. I fear something will crack, allowing grief to creep back in like a fog and take over.

It's a place I try to avoid. It's so hard to crawl back out. So, I keep it at arm's length.

Please don't take it personally.

My actions are not based on judgment or ego. I'm simply trying to survive a loss.

I hope you know how precious every moment is. It is my wish that the look of unknowing innocence always remains behind your eyes.

Sincerely,
This Bereaved Mother

Chapter 10

People Surprise You

You learn a lot about other people when your child dies.

I shared our story publicly. In doing that, I created much needed conversation around child loss and grief. I reminded people not to take their loved ones for granted. I also allowed complete strangers into our most intimate moments.

I do not regret our decision to share, not for a single second; but people can be "fun".

One woman told me I was a horrible mother because of the impossible decisions I made on the day Cameron died. While my son was literally laying in a hospital bed dying, I went home to "celebrate Christmas" with my daughter. She had never lost a child, but she knew what it should look like. At least, she *thought* she did.

I've had countless people tell me they hope my son found Jesus; otherwise, he never made it to heaven.

Another woman told me I needed to see a psychiatrist, because the truths I was sharing about the realities of child loss were a clear demonstration that I was no longer in touch with reality. It was obvious to her it was a cry for help and everyone in my life was simply ignoring it.

Again, she was not a bereaved mother. She had no clue.

I'm sorry if the reality of life after child loss is too much for you. Actually, that's why I share. We need to normalize the experience. Too often, people think the things we say and do are signs that we need help. Nothing I have ever shared even borders on psychotic behavior; but thanks for your concern. Stick to the stuff you know.

Then, there are the people you know who abandon their deli meat order at the grocery store to run for the checkout, because having a simple, two-minute conversation with you (not even in reference to Cameron) is just too much for them to bear.

Sometimes there are people that do the opposite, like Ruthie.

I met her for the first time at Cameron's memorial. She showed up wearing her brand-new baby and towing 3 other children with her. Each of them wore a superhero shirt, and I knew she had likely gone out of her way to buy them specifically for this event.

I recognized her, but only because one of her daughters was in Cameron's first grade class. I had gathered in the same general proximity every day at school pickup. Our only prior interaction would have been a smile or a simple hello in passing.

She pulled me aside to tell me Cameron's name was one of the first she had heard in her home. They were new to town. She told me it was unusual for her daughter to remember names and talk about kids from school, so it was a big deal when she came home and mentioned my son.

As our conversation came to a close, she asked if I would meet her for breakfast on Monday when the kids returned to school after Christmas break. She went on to tell me she had experienced multiple miscarriages and, while it may not compare to my loss, she understood the need to have people around who got it. She then insisted, saying it could be a good distraction for a short while.

I took the bait. Something made me say yes.

That was the start of an unexpected friendship. One I had no idea how much I would need in that first year. Not only did she just show up without asking what I needed, but she went out of her way to be there. A text before she left for the store to see if she could pick something up for me. Lunch dates during the week. A random card in the mail with a joke to make me laugh.

She dove headfirst into the hard conversations. There had been a scene in a movie that referenced death, after which, she had pulled me aside to see how it hit me and if I was OK. A comment someone had made, innocently, but she brought it up to let me know she heard it and knew. She was so keenly aware of the things no one else seemed to notice.

Then there was Monica. Living on the opposite side of the country didn't keep her from showing up. Not only did she leave her family on Christmas to fly to me when she heard the news, but she surprised me with all the things I needed to collect memories from everyone who attended Cameron's memorial.

She knew having these memories was important to me. One of my biggest fears was forgetting anything. On her last night with us, she stayed up all night to execute on her plan. I had no clue! That next morning, I woke up to a text telling me everything I needed was on the front porch.

Monica continued showing up. Each week, we had a standing phone date. She took the burden of being the one to initiate the calls and text messages. I am forever grateful to her for not shying away from the uncomfortable. Every week, she gave me the space to talk or not to talk. She never tried to fix me. Instead, she sought to understand and made sure Cameron's name and memories easily flowed in the conversation. That meant everything!

And then there was Tracy. I joke that she only brought misery, because she convinced me to start running, a thing I swore I would never do; but it helped tremendously in my early grief.

Her son was my son's best friend at school. She and I had only exchanged numbers and talked a couple of times. We waved at school drop off in the mornings. Our boys had not yet fully brought us together.

When Cameron died, she told me a part of her felt like she had missed an opportunity to know us; but she didn't. She inserted herself into our lives. She became one of those people who isn't just a friend, but someone who does life with you. She remembers Cameron's birthday, talks openly about him with her son, and always acknowledges the hole that exists.

It is often the people you least expect that make the biggest impact.

Let me tell you about Tammy.

It was almost one year and eight months after the death of my son when I got a message that would show me the ripple effect his death had created. It said, "You don't know me... not really. We have met – once. You see, I was the 'other' nurse."

She was the one that came in and took charge during the shift change. I told her I remembered the shift change, but the faces were blurry, as I was quite distracted by that point. I also went on to say that it was nice to know, in a sea of patients, we were remembered. It sounded horrible, but doesn't everything now?

She said, "Remembered would be an understatement."

We connected. We cried together on the phone. She had been a total stranger.

That night, when she entered the room, my son was already in a coma. He was being prepped for his spinal tap. I didn't know it at the time, but she was immediately sent to our room upon arrival that morning, skipping her pre-shift meeting, because she had prior experience working in pediatrics, and we needed her.

The first thing she did as she entered the room was assess my son and ask me if she could cut his shirt off. She needed to be able to see his breathing. Of course, I said yes.

In this phone conversation, she revealed what I never saw or knew.

In my world, post Cameron's death, every time I would see a Captain America shirt, it would haunt me. It was the shirt we put on him before driving to the hospital. The shirt they cut off him. It was worn often. Not because it was a superhero shirt, simply because I loved how it fit him. It was my favorite.

When Tammy had asked if it was OK to cut it off, I didn't hesitate. "Yes, do whatever you need to do."

It was the last time I saw it.

In Tammy's world, every time she saw a Captain America shirt, it would haunt her.

She remembered.

When she entered the room early that morning, she was concerned he was still wearing a shirt. Apparently, one of the first things you are taught in pediatrics for these situations is to remove the clothing so you can see if there is any strain (watching their ribs) as a child tries to breathe.

That hadn't been done. So, she did what was necessary.

She told me as her scissors cut through the shirt, she couldn't stop thinking, "I just cut his shield... his protection."

We didn't know it at the time, but an hour after she cut it, he would be unable to come back to us.

Her story didn't stop there. She went on to tell me that she had called the children's hospital after her shift to get an update and see how Cameron was doing.

When they told her the news, she immediately drove back to work and demanded all the trash from the ER that night so she could dig through it and search for the shirt.

It was never found.

She spent more than a year searching for an exact replica of that shirt!

Every time she passed a boys' clothing section, she would stop and look. She knew that the only way to make things right in the universe was to find a replacement and get it to me; but not just any replacement! It had to be the same coloring and style.

None of the shirts she came across were right. In an attempt to ease her mind, she bought a Pandora charm that was a Captain America shield. She held onto it. Then, one day, she came upon a replica that was pretty darn close. That's when she contacted me and told me she had a gift for me.

She knew the time was right when she had both the charm and the shirt.

I always wear that charm on my necklace, along with his handwriting and a fingerprint. It not only connects me to that day, but it serves as a reminder that he made an impact!

She told me she would never forget Cameron. She remembered his name and was not afraid to speak it. It made my day, my week, my month, my whole year!

The surprises didn't end there. Completely unrelated, I heard from Beth. She works as a nurse at the children's hospital. She was not one of his nurses, but her husband was in the back of the ambulance with Cameron. When we arrived and climbed out of the ambulance, he met me as I came around the back. He was the one who had drawn the short stick and was tasked with telling me things had changed.

Another moment burned into my brain, but without a face.

Beth told me her husband, Steve, said he would never forget that moment and hated to have to deliver that news. It had broken his heart.

In a strange way, that meant so much to hear. We were not just a number.

Even five years after Cameron's death, Beth informed me that she had shared our story with a new nurse on her floor. She always remembered us.

There is something about a complete stranger thinking about your child, remembering them, that fills your soul with warmth and love. He mattered! He left an imprint.

The ripple effect that came from the death of our child was enormous. It continues to exist beyond our ability to comprehend, because it has touched so many people in ways we can't see.

Our stories not only keep them alive, but they inspire renewed gratitude, extra hugs, kind words, and random acts of kindness. Each one creates a positive push of love into the world that keeps on going.

There is so much power in telling our stories! Not only does it help create healing within us, but it helps those on this same journey, struggling to find their way forward.

When you share a story or memory with us, it is everything! We may cry, or we may not; but that part is insignificant. The simple fact that someone speaks of our child and reminds us they are not forgotten allows us to feel loved and seen! That is worth everything to us!

Chapter 11

I Used To Be A Better Mom

I used to be a better mom… before.

That is not a statement I make so that people will disagree and compliment me. It is simply the truth.

There is nothing that makes you feel more inadequate than parenting after loss.

I no longer knew how to care for myself… what I needed. How was I supposed to care for my children? My son died on my watch. *Died.* I'm pretty sure that immediately classified me as "questionable", at best.

When people find out your child died, you know their first thought is, "What happened?" Even that night, at the hospital, I felt the judgement as doctors probed me, trying to figure out what I had done, what he had done. Things didn't add up, and that always casts a black shadow of doubt.

We still had two daughters at home. Together, they fueled our survival. It's hard to stay in bed all day when you have young kids who need you and no family nearby. So, we fell into a pattern that looked like life.

To the outside world, it resembled normal. We returned to the daily routine of school after Christmas break. We packed lunches and did homework. We watched a baby crawl, then walk, then run. We celebrated birthdays and holidays. We mowed the grass, did the laundry, and checked the boxes that made it seem like we were moving forward.

But it felt so empty. It was so different; not normal. I know the girls felt it, too.

We were going through the motions. The whole "fake it until you make it", but we weren't really making it; and we weren't good at faking it, either.

My husband and I used distraction tactics to balance the pain. We spent a lot of time binge watching shows I don't even remember. Our emotional, mental, and physical energy levels were completely depleted. There was nothing there.

It felt like drawing straws each time one of the girls needed something. Who would draw the short straw this time? And it took every ounce of energy to do the most basic, mundane things.

It was in these moments I knew I had become a bad mom. More guilt bubbled up.

This isn't what motherhood should look like. It isn't what I had envisioned. It isn't what I used to do, but I couldn't begin to make a change. I just couldn't. It felt impossible.

Grief brings with it an inability to do many things. *I can't* is a real concept! There were so many things I just could no longer do. It seemed ridiculous, but they were physically impossible.

I could no longer get on the floor and play with my daughters. It's what Cameron did.

I could no longer read books to them. They had belonged to Cameron, first.

I could no longer create special nights or plan surprises.

I felt myself pull back from anything that resembled making memories.

There were no overwhelming feelings of gratitude for what I still had. No increased wave of emotion, pushing me to grab a hold of my daughters and not let go. Instead, I just felt nothing. I was numb.

My love for my daughters was still there. Daily, I would remind myself that even though I felt void of everything, they still meant everything! I was broken.

When they would get sick, I immediately went into "worst-case scenario" mode. A simple fever would push me over the edge. I was terrified it was porphyria. Cameron's autopsy had shown signs of past trauma, something we weren't aware of until that report. I couldn't come up with anything except what we considered "normal sick". How was I supposed to be able to tell the difference now?

When my kids would act up or I would see certain behaviors, I would question whether this was a grief response from losing their brother or was this just normal kid stuff? Navigating that was hard. I was so unable to decipher these behaviors that I started taking my oldest daughter to a therapist. I needed a second set of eyes. Someone who could assure me that I wasn't screwing things up. Someone who could also help me handle some of the things we had going on.

Modeling healthy grief is important. It's not something I felt equipped to do. There is a fine line between letting them see you experience grief and scaring the hell out of them as they witness you struggling in the darkest place you've ever been.

Emotions are something I always felt very disconnected from. I didn't know how to regulate them. How to properly identify them. Most importantly, how to process them. I really felt most comfortable shoving them back in and finding a way over them.

This is what I had modeled to my children, without even realizing it.

Our first experiences with death shape how we handle grief and loss. Unfortunately, loss is a big part of life, even beyond death. This was their first, and I had made mistakes.

About a month after Cameron died, my oldest daughter unexpectedly asked, "Would you be this sad if it was me who had died?"

Talk about feeling like I was hit by a train! It was out of the blue. Her words were so honest, raw… and they stung. This was proof we were failing her. To all of the people who had said, "At least you still have your girls…" Yes, they kept us going and gave us something to live for; but they can't fill the hole. Nothing can.

My family never feels complete. I always see what is missing. While I am forever thankful to still have them, it does not make the situation better. It just *is* the situation.

This is our reality. We went from a family of five to looking like a family of four. We can't reconcile that change. We will forever be missing a physical piece.

My daughter's words did change us, though. They had forced us to reflect on the things outside of our own perspective. We saw her grief. We saw our attempts to "fake it until you make it" through her eyes.

Not only had my girls lost their big brother, but they also lost both of their parents. With him went a big piece of each of us. They didn't deserve this new mom or dad. They had experienced enough loss when their brother disappeared from their life.

I learned how to dig deeper.

I started making changes with what I called "Hail Marys".

These were activities like a surprise day of hiking to go geocaching, a movie date, or a spontaneous trip to play mini golf.

The mom I used to be would jam pack our long weekends, spring breaks, and summer vacations full of exciting outings and surprises. We would have fun! Now, I just felt like I was always letting them down.

So, I would go for the Hail Mary. Right at the end, a last-ditch effort to change the narrative and give them some enjoyment.

I got really good at throwing things together at the last minute to create entertainment for the girls. Spontaneity is a skill I use often. I embraced the fact that we were making memories and began looking for my son in those moments.

He shows up. I see echoes of him in our memories, and I cherish them.

It will never be exactly the same as it was before, but such is life after loss.

A little voice told me it was OK. It's the effort that counts, the intent. As long as I kept making the effort, I knew it would all work out.

Chapter 12

The Number Twelve

My son died in the twelfth month, just after midnight.

I didn't know it yet, but this number would soon hold a lot of meaning.

In the early months of grief, I found myself glancing at the clock multiple times throughout the day. The minutes would almost always be 12.

I took notice. However, I hadn't quite bought into the idea that there was real meaning there; but it kept happening. There were times my phone would beep. I would pick it up and see the time, minutes at 12, but no messages or other reason for the phone to make a sound.

That was a little weird.

Then, I started to notice a lot of 12s had been woven into our lives. It was as if the universe had placed them there so that when this happened, I would notice the trend and it would help open the door for communication.

I was born in the twelfth month. My son's due date was October 12th, though he was born early, via c-section. He weighed 9 pounds, 12.5 ounces at birth. We had made a major move across the country in 2012.

That one was hard, because I had started to believe that if we had never moved, he would never have come in contact with whatever had caused his illness. He would still be alive. That wasn't true. The guilt in that was heavy, and later I realized they were all lies I had told myself.

The 12s kept coming.

When I shared our story publicly, the post went viral. I was inundated with comments and messages from complete strangers. They were moved by my vulnerability. Many saw pieces of their own story. No one talks about child loss. When they do, it's not in such an intimate way.

One of those strangers was the mother of a child who happened to be in the PICU room next to us that night. The world is a very small place.

In her message to me, she expressed her condolences. She said they were in room 2014. That night, they knew a child had died, but they didn't know the details surrounding it. She saw me exit his room and fall apart for the first time since arriving at the children's hospital. It was difficult for her to see and it took everything inside of her not to walk into the hall and wrap me in a hug. She didn't want to invade my privacy.

Of course, I was completely oblivious to everything going on around me.

What I found most strange was my preoccupation with her room number as I read her message. I have no idea why, but my immediate thought was, "I wonder what room number we were in?"

I had to have that answer. So, I dug into his medical records, which if you've lost a child and have had to read medical records or autopsy reports, you know what a rabbit hole of torture they are.

There it was, in plain black and white. We were in room 2012. Weird.

When I had reconnected with one of Cameron's nurses, Tammy, she told me that night, when he had become emergent and they moved us into a larger room before our hospital transfer, we were moved into room 12.

I flipped through old family photos and watched videos. I was trying to organize him, his life, into a folder. I wanted to be able to access it all without digging through everything else. I came upon an old photo of him. The summer he was 4, we had signed him up to play flag football. His jersey was #12.

There were others. During school drop off, I noticed the number above his old classroom was 112.

I felt like this number was everywhere I turned. I didn't tell anyone that I had started to question if this number had been placed here throughout our lives for me to notice later, to guide me to something bigger. It felt like a really strange thing to contemplate. At that time, I wasn't even sure I believed it was possible. Yet, the evidence just kept mounting.

Most people would tell me that if I wanted to see 12s, my subconscious would look for them and bring them to my attention. It was a self-fulfilling prophecy of sorts. This was not that. I knew it.

That next week, my mom came to visit. She needed to put eyes on us and make sure we were doing OK.

On one of the first days of her visit, we decided to grab lunch before picking up my oldest daughter from school. We went to a little diner. The woman at the front seated us at a table in the corner. As we sat down, a little card with the table number on it literally fell out of its holder and flopped onto the table right in front of me.

Table 12!

I had a visceral reaction and gasped, "Oh, my god! It's a 12!"

I'm pretty sure my Mom thought I was going crazy. The server was worried and asked if it was OK. I assured her it was fine, and she left. Then, I proceeded to walk my mom through my 12 theory.

A couple of weeks went by before the next 12 showed up.

There was a local festival in town. We had never gone to it before. These were the things I used to do as a mother. Doing them now was difficult because of the constant reminder of how things used to be and the sadness of making new memories without him. I was feeling really guilty though, because my oldest daughter was missing out. I needed to step it up for her. So, she and I went.

Parking was very limited for this event. We had to park in a lot across town and be bussed to the location. She was beyond excited, because this would be her first bus ride. I was focused on the fact it was something Cameron always wanted to do, but he didn't get to.

She led the way and picked out our seat. As we settled in, my mind drifted to a mother and son chatting in a seat nearby. I could hear him telling her all about where he sits on his bus. He called out the row number, and they looked back to find it.

In that moment, I wondered what seat we were in. I looked up to see seat 12. It made me smile.

Our first trip to the movie theater, the local ads filled the screen while we waited for the feature to begin. The last ad we saw before the lights went down was sports themed. It ended with the camera panning into the dugout, focusing on the back of a little boy with jersey #12. I knew Cameron was there with us. He loved the movies!

These 12s are not coincidence. I no longer believe in coincidence. They are his way of saying "Hi!", of letting me know he is still around for it all. It's his way of sending us a hug and a smile and validating the things we are doing.

He was becoming a guide, of sorts, reassuring me the things we were doing were as they should be, and I was filled with love and gratitude.

These 12s have continued as the years have moved on.

I had a minor health scare that required an ER visit. We drove to the other side of town so as to avoid the triggers of the hospital from that dreadful night. As the nurse escorted me back to a room, I saw the number. As we walked in, I said, "Room 12?" She said, "Yeah, is that OK?" I explained to her the significance and knew he was right there with me.

My youngest daughter has ADHD. We had scheduled an evaluation with a behavioral analyst to help guide us on things that can support her learning challenges. It was a time when I was advocating really hard for people to see her struggles and it was difficult finding the support we needed.

During the meeting, she paused to tell me a story about her child. Of all the stories she could have selected, it was a story about how her daughter used to struggle with saying the word twelve. TWELVE?! I knew that was Cameron's way of saying I was on the right path. He was right!

In that next month, we finally had a provider see her! It was during that evaluation that we got the answers we were seeking. The diagnoses have helped open doors for treatment plans and support she will need going forward.

For my grandmother's 80th birthday, we traveled out of state to attend a surprise party with family. These weekends are hard, because the distraction of being out of our normal surroundings, being inundated with people, often leads to a grief setback, or a surge of grief when I return home.

On the drive home, I began to reflect on the fact that my connection to Cameron felt strained in those situations. They require me to hold extra space for him, which is delicate to balance.

My attention then shifted to the radio. Driving down the highway, I heard "I Don't Want to Miss a Thing" by Aerosmith. This is the song that had played in my head the final 12 hours of his life, as I had tried to process the fact he would soon be gone.

That song immediately takes me back, beside him in that bed, watching him breathe. I was so exhausted. I was doing everything in my power to not fall asleep beside him, because those moments were far too precious to sleep through.

As I tuned in to what the song meant, my GPS instructed me to exit and stay right. So, I did.

My thoughts focused on the fact I hadn't been able to find him during the weekend, as I usually did. It bothered me.

The voice on the GPS broke through, telling me to stay left in the fork. I looked at the screen to see "rerouting". My brain couldn't process fast enough, so I quickly switched lanes, just in time to realize I was now going the wrong way.

Thanks to that reroute, I was traveling north when I needed to be traveling south. As my route recalculated again, I was told to take the next exit to make my u-turn. It was Exit 12.

I cannot explain to you how or why my GPS rerouted me when it did. I know it sounds like a huge coincidence that the next exit was 12. All I can tell you is I jokingly scolded my son, blaming him for the detour. "You couldn't have just flashed a 12 on the clock?!"

He wanted to make sure I was paying attention. Reassuring me that even though I didn't "find him" over the weekend, he was still there.

He is always there!

Chapter 13

I Saw Him

When your child dies, you suddenly *have to* know where they went. Whatever beliefs you carried your entire life, they are no longer good enough. You have to *know*!

Well, I found my son pretty quickly.

It started about 3 weeks after Cameron died.

From the corner of my eye, a shadow of movement streaked across the balcony above my kitchen. I looked up, half expecting to see one of my kids playing, but the balcony was empty. There was no one there.

I turned my attention back to the sink full of dirty dishes and continued scrubbing. A few moments passed. There it was again! My eyes diverted up and quickly scanned the entire length of the balcony, but nothing had changed. What was that? Am I going crazy?

By this time, I started questioning my sanity. My mind started saying, "I swear I'm seeing Cameron. It's like he's running from one end to the other and slipping behind the wall to hide as I look up." But, my son died last month. That's not even possible! Or is it?

I am here to tell you that nothing about child loss is mainstream! Nothing is what you would expect it to be. You are broken wide open and suddenly all the things you believed no longer make sense. You experience things you never thought possible; but they are.

A few days passed. Again, I found myself standing at the kitchen sink. This time, the shadow drew my attention to the other side of the room. Standing directly in front of his urn was the full figure shadow of my son. His exact size and shape.

I gasped. My hands grabbed the edge of the counter to steady my balance. Almost as quickly as I saw it, the shadow vanished into mist. It was gone. I had no idea what was going on, but my mind was reeling. That was Cameron!

A couple more weeks passed. I had told no one about seeing the shadows because I knew how crazy it would sound. People would assume I was a grieving mother who would do anything to connect to her son. Her mind must be playing tricks. I had moments I started to believe it myself.

Then, validation came!

My husband and I went to our first medium. He jumped through hoops so she wouldn't know our identities or have any opportunity to research us ahead of time. He had a colleague in another state schedule the appointment. She never gave our name or details about who we hoped to connect with. She even used her own credit card for payment.

There was no way she could find out anything about us prior to walking in the door.

Near the end of the session, she looked right at me and said, "You've been seeing shadows."

My husband skeptically replied with a no, while my jaw hit the floor! My head slowly shaking, I said, "Yes... I have." His head snapped in my direction, bewildered at my response. "You have?"

Before I could respond, she said, "Those shadows you see are your son. He loves to run now that he is free of the restrictions we have here on earth. He can run so much faster and loves running through your house."

I just smiled.

She then added, "You're also seeing a number over and over." Validation for the number 12. Again, my husband had no clue. She told me my son would use that number to send messages. That validation moved me from believing it may be possible it was him to *knowing* it was him.

He was sending me a clear message he is still here. While his physical body is gone, he is very much present. Life goes on after death.

More than a year passed before I saw him again. This time, I was standing at my bathroom sink getting ready for bed. I saw a shadow in the mirror streak behind me, directly over my right shoulder. I swung around, half expecting to see one of my daughters standing there. I was alone.

There was no doubt in my mind it was him. I knew he was running. Like last time, I just knew.

At the time of writing this book, I have seen him once more.

It was late. My room was dark, aside from my closet light. I always left the light on with the door cracked. It had become a habit after caring for 3 children who would get up at all hours of the night.

As I laid in bed, scrolling social media before sleep, I saw a full-scale child's shadow appear on the wall across from my closet and walk into my room. Except, no child came with it.

I sat up straight and then climbed out of bed in search of that child, softly calling out to my living daughter. Again, I fully expected to see her standing in the hallway. Nothing! I even went so far as to continue walking to her room where I found her, sound asleep in bed.

I knew what I had seen; but I needed to eliminate any other potential causes. The entrance to my bedroom is a hallway. My closet was the only source of light, so I knew someone had to cross in front of it to cast that shadow. There was no physical source that could explain the shadow I saw. I know it was Cameron.

Not only have I seen him, but I have felt him.

Thinking back on that first morning after his death, I realized my son had come to me.

It happened just after 6 AM, the way it had every morning that last year of his life. He would quietly walk into my room and stand beside my bed. His body would ever so slightly graze the mattress right at my shoulder and the motion would wake me.

I always opened my eyes to find his smiling face, asking if he could play video games.

That morning, I jolted awake, confused. Hoping to see him standing beside me, I wondered if this was all just a horrible dream. Nothing. There was no one there.

I grabbed my phone beside the bed to see the time. "He should be waking me up right now."

At the time, I didn't realize he was showing up to let me know he was still there.

Then there was the time I felt his hand on my arm.

Again, I was asleep in bed. As I laid on my right side, sound asleep, a hand rested on my left arm. The physical touch was enough to gently wake me. The room was dark. I rolled onto my back to see who was standing beside my bed, trying to wake me. There was no one there.

These instances I speak of weren't scary in any way. They were comforting, as if they were the most normal things in the world, real, physical experiences.

Many people write these things off as my imagination. A grieving mother, desperate to maintain a connection with her son, something that must be explained away because it just isn't logical.

I know better.

Very little in the grief experience aligns with mainstream thinking. The things you see, feel, and think can make you feel like you are going crazy. This is part of the reason people don't talk about them; but not talking about these experiences doesn't make them any less real. Nobody gets it until it happens to them.

There is no doubt in my mind that death is not the end. Sure, their physical body has died. Yet, they continue to exist, just in a new way. They are not "looking down on us", "in our hearts", or in some faraway place. They are close enough that if we reached out our hand, we could touch them.

They continue to walk this journey with us, seeing us, hearing us, knowing. They support us in our journey forward. Love never dies! We just have to be willing to look outside of what we used to think of as normal to find them.

Chapter 14

Our Relationship Continues

I had always been fascinated by "other worldly" things, even to the point that I would say I believed the stories that I had heard were real. Though when I had heard a voice myself, I still had a tiny part of me that would wonder how much of it was true.

I tell people my son's death fueled a need to know; but in reality, the proof just showed up, in my face, making it nearly impossible not to believe.

The number 12, the shadows... there have been countless other signs.

People tend to assume I am super religious because of the way I talk about belief that Cameron walks beside me and sends me signs; but I am not. In fact, I don't even consider myself a Christian. I grew up in the church, but organized religion never resonated with me. It always felt man made.

This thing that I was experiencing was so much bigger.

For his 8th birthday, our first birthday without him physically here, he made his presence known. I was set on celebrating as we always did. At the party store, I purchased a dozen balloons as I always had done when we would celebrate one of the kids' birthdays.

In those early years, we did a balloon release. One each balloon was a little note with a personal email address, should anyone find a balloon and wish to respond. Family and friends all over the country joined us in remembering Cameron.

That year, we received exactly 8 messages back.

The first gave hope to a couple who had just been told they would need fertility treatments to start a family. The second didn't provide any details, but we know it was found locally. The third was found on a beach in Michigan. The fourth was found by a family with an 8-year-old child, just like Cameron would have been. The fifth was found in a baseball field. The person had tied it to the back fence, only to find it in his yard the next morning. He knew, then, he had to message us. The sixth was found by a family out for a hike on their property. It was off the trail and their 11-year-old son knew they needed to email. The seventh found its way to a farm hand, working in the field. He credited his great day to Cameron.

The last balloon was the most touching. It was found by a bereaved mother. Her 19-year-old son had also died in December. She said this year was the first year they were going to be able to enjoy Christmas again, because they were first-time grandparents.

For his 9th birthday, I again purchased balloons. That year, Cameron had jokes!

I handed my list to the cashier, who began pulling them, one by one, to create a pile for the order. A red balloon dropped on top of the pile and caught my eye, but something didn't make sense, and I did a double take. It said, "Welcome Back".

Welcome back?! In my head, I immediately said, "I wish."

I pulled it off the pile, as I held back my inappropriate chuckle, and relayed that that one was a mistake. While it seemed completely morbid, I loved it.

Cameron always had understood sarcasm, even at a very early age. It always had a place in our home before his death. It deserved a place after, as well. He obviously agreed.

I ultimately went back and bought that balloon as #13 because I couldn't ignore the opportunity to share another inside joke with my son.

The night before his birthday, two balloons were droopy. There was no way they would last. I jokingly said to my husband, "Wouldn't it be funny if we had exactly 9 balloons to send him on his 9th birthday?"

In the morning, we awoke to find three of the balloons on the floor. We had ten remaining.

I kid you not, as I went to grab the balloons for our release, we watched one literally fall to the floor!

We ended up with only 9 balloons that would fly that day. The craziest part was, we had selected all his favorite characters and then filled in with colored shapes for the rest. All non-character balloons were "lost". Cameron's launch included only his favorite characters. I guess he didn't want the others.

These signs turned into a game we played.

One afternoon, sitting at my kitchen table, I noticed a balloon hovering above the balcony in our kitchen. Like a crazy person, I snapped a photo and asked Cameron to please bring it to me. No one else was around. I was alone.

I watched for a few minutes as it bobbed around. Then, I got up to leave the room for only a minute. When I returned, there it was, hovering at face level, one foot from where I had been sitting. I can't explain it.

I even asked him to send me a balloon that had been released in memory of someone else. I wanted to see what it felt like to find one.

During the pandemic, my daughters and I made a trip to the hardware store. As we exited the car and walked toward the store entrance, I watched a red heart balloon gently drift from the sky and land on the sidewalk in front of us. On the balloon was written a note, sending love to their Granddaddy on his birthday.

I know how these stories sound! They are so crazy I can't even make them up.

My relationship with Cameron seemed to grow and continue. It blew my mind. We were still connected and could somehow communicate.

The idea for the game originated from a video I had watched. A well-known medium, Laura Lynn Jackson, was doing a reading on a morning show. In it, she had said to "ask for a really specific sign, something you wouldn't normally come across, like a purple elephant. As validation, ask your loved one to send it to you. Then, open yourself up to receive it."

So, I call it the Purple Elephant game.

My husband is a skeptic. He can reason away anything that doesn't make logical sense. Even still, he hopes to receive his own signs.

On our way to trick-or-treat one year, I told him about the video. I explained all he needed to do was ask for a purple elephant. The key? He needed to open himself up to receive it, not reason it all away. He was very noncommittal, so I asked!

I asked Cameron to send me a purple elephant. I knew he would. I just needed to be patient.

I've learned that these things don't always happen right away. They certainly won't happen the way you think they will; but they do happen! You just have to be open to seeing them.

At trick-or-treat, there were no purple elephants. That was fine with me. He could have too easily written it off as being Halloween.

However, a couple of nights later, it happened! I was in the kitchen, cooking dinner. My oldest daughter turned the TV on for my youngest daughter. *Paw Patrol* became our background noise. As I looked up to tell them dinner was ready, there it was, on the screen, my purple elephant!

I screamed for the girls to hit the pause button! I took a picture to send as proof to my husband.

My son also sends me hearts, and my daughters get pennies.

On one of these occasions, I was out running errands. The first stop took me to the dollar store. While there, I picked up a new loofah for the bathroom.

I reached into the bin and dug for green. It was Cameron's favorite color, so that's what we buy. As I pulled it out, I told him, "Green for you."

Walking to my car to load the bags, there was a penny on the ground. It was a little destroyed, but a penny. Usually, he only sends these to the girls, but I snapped a picture and picked it up.

Next on the list was the hardware store. Walking the aisles, I thought about how people who don't understand signs scoff that it's just a penny, a mere coincidence, not from Cameron, or a loved one, only something to make us think of them.

They are wrong.

Leaving the hardware store, I walked to the back of my car to unload my bags. There on the ground was a heart, in the exact location I had found the penny earlier. I snapped a picture.

Back in the car, I told Cameron that the things he was doing were helping to convince others that their loved ones were still there, too.

On my way home, I stopped to grab dinner. Next to the drink machine were two pennies. One for each of my daughters, because he sends them pennies. He wanted to make sure they each got one.

When my youngest daughter turned 5, the girls spent the evening before her birthday in the pool. They swam until long after the sun went down. Night swimming was always a favorite for my kids. They would turn the light on, everything turned green.

The next morning, on her birthday, I almost walked into a huge spider web in our back pool area, right by the light switch. It wasn't there the night before. In the middle of the web was a heart. I couldn't believe it. He was letting us know he was there.

Recently, we got rid of an older car. It was the very first car my husband and I had purchased brand new. When Cameron was really little, he would tell us how much he loved that car. When he turned 16, it would be his. I always joked there was no way he would want anything to do with that car when he turned 16.

Now, we will never know.

In later years, the car sat in our driveway. It was our "just in case" vehicle. We barely drove it.

The night Cameron got sick, I drove him to the hospital in that car. It made sense because my husband had the baby. Her car seat easily snapped into the car we always drove. So, my husband carried Cameron to the car as I grabbed my purse.

He was propped in the front seat beside me. Mostly so I could keep an eye on him, but also it allowed me to help him hold the bucket in case he got sick again.

That night, we hit every single green light. It was a game we used to play. See if we can make it to our destination without the car coming to a full stop. That night we almost succeeded. As the light next to the hospital entrance turned red, he said, "We are so lucky. This was the only red light we hit."

We weren't lucky at all. That night would just go from bad to worse.

Years after, that car would sit in our driveway. It became our third car… one we never drove and would take a beating in the Florida sun. Still, I couldn't get rid of it. Too many memories attached to it.

That is, until recently. One of the things I've learned is that I no longer necessarily need the things to retain the memories. Sometimes, those things no longer serve a purpose, and you realize it's time to release them.

We found a company to haul it away. As I cleaned out the car for the last time, there in the cupholder was one lonely penny. The year on the penny was 2012. A twelve! In the backseat was one lonely heart sticker.

He was letting me know that he knew, and it was OK.

He still plays the red light game with us. One afternoon, we were headed to the other side of town for lunch. We almost always hit a ton of red lights on our drive there. This day was different. We breezed through the first two.

As we approached the third light, everyone was aware there was a pattern forming, and the game was on! With each green light, the energy in the car increased. The girls were yelling from the back, "Come on, keep the lights green".

We must have cruised on through 15 different traffic lights without a single stop. We were coming up on our last light. Everyone in the car was screaming at the light to change; but it didn't. As everyone hollered their disappointment, I noticed the license plate in front of us. The last 3 digits were 012. Cameron's way of letting us know he was right there, screaming with us.

Christmas is always a tough time for us. As the rest of the world seems to count down to their favorite holiday, we recount our worst.

Shopping during this time of year is especially tough. All the gifts we should be purchasing. The non-stop reminders. Going out into the holiday chaos usually requires a pep talk.

That particular year, I was headed out for some dreaded shopping. Pulling out of our driveway, I said to my son, "Help me out, Cameron. Let this be a productive trip."

At my destination, I started to pull into a parking spot. There was a person climbing into their car, so I kept driving to the next open spot. The moment I turned in, I saw it.

Right in front of me was a license plate that said LOVE CAM. It was like a big "Hello!" Cameron was letting me know he was right there, always listening.

Then, there was the night my mother-in-law died. The girls and I were with friends at our weekly game of family trivia. We got the text from my husband as we were paying our bill to leave.

As my daughter stood up, she found 2 pennies on the back of the booth. There was no way they were there when we arrived. The kids were constantly up and down, climbing in and out. We would have seen them; but there they were, letting us know Cameron and Grandma were together.

Our loved ones are still here. They aren't hanging out in some faraway place "watching over us". They are right here with us. Give them a chance and they will show up.

While these signs are amazing and the continuation of our relationship helps, it in no way replaces our yearning to have them here, physically with us. I will take what I can get!

Chapter 15

Medium Readings Saved Me

Yep, I said it. Medium readings were a total game-changer for me.

People worry it is evil. I assure you, it is not. Every reading I've had, every message that has come through, is full of love.

The bigger win has been how these experiences have given me the confidence to trust my own intuition. That confidence has allowed me to trust the messages I have been getting from Cameron.

It all started with my very first medium reading, two months after Cameron's death. My anxiety was through the roof. This was the make-or-break moment. I had always believed before, at least I thought I had. Still, there was a part of me that was terrified he wouldn't come through and I had been wrong.

He definitely showed up! She told me things I hadn't even said out loud: the shadows I was seeing; the number 12, over and over. She even told me about a miscarriage my mom had, that I knew nothing about, but confirmed with my mom after our reading.

She blew my mind! Every fear I had had evaporated. I knew I was still connected to my son.

After our reading, I sent her a message, asking what books she recommended. I needed to know what it's like where he is now. What happens when we die? How do I strengthen my connection with my son?

She invited me to attend a workshop she had coming up in the next few weeks. It was a beginner mediumship training. The idea was that we all can connect. It is through practice and meditation that you develop the skill. Again, something I had always believed. I just never had a reason to go there.

It was a small group of women. Almost every single person in that room was well beyond me from a skill level. I felt more like a fly on the wall playing games while watching them hone their skills. It was fun.

At lunch, one of the women shared something with the group. The night before our workshop, she received a message. From it, she knew she would meet a bereaved mother at the event (there were only two of us in the group). The message was for one of us.

In her message, she kept getting an image of Minnie Mouse. We all laughed, because we were in Orlando. She assured us it had nothing to do with Disney World and being in Orlando. Yet, she didn't have any other details to reference.

It didn't resonate with either of us, so we filed it away and moved on.

Leading up to that first Christmas after Cameron's death, some of my best friends organized a reindeer drive in honor of Cameron. His absolute favorite thing in the world was his stuffed reindeer, appropriately named, Reindeer. We had people in multiple cities collecting stuffed reindeer, with a plan to deliver them to children in the hospital at Christmastime.

Here locally, our little school was a drop-off zone. Friends were handling the logistics of delivering everything to the children's hospital, the same place Cameron had died.

It just so happened that their drop off appointment was scheduled on the same day my daughter had one of her appointments at the hospital. It was completely random, as our appointment had been on the calendar for six months. They had no idea of our schedule until after the drop-off day was booked.

We were going to be at the hospital when they delivered Cameron's reindeer. It was a total coincidence, though there are none. I politely declined participation, because it was too much for me to handle.

My daughter's appointment was my first time back at the hospital. Walking past the door we had exited that night. Passing the elevators we had used to get to the PICU. Knowing that the second story was only level above me. It was rough!

Our appointment was a full day, due to imaging in the morning and the doctor's visit after lunch. Our friends made their reindeer delivery and then met us on the playground. This is where Minnie Mouse made her entrance.

During the reindeer drive, someone local had made a donation that also included a Minnie Mouse doll. As they tagged reindeer for distribution, they decided not to include Minnie. Instead, they felt it was something my girls should have. After all, it wasn't a reindeer.

I never told anyone about the Minnie Mouse message I had gotten several months before.

Had Cameron really asked me to file Minnie Mouse away in the back of my mind so that I would recognize his gift to them on their first Christmas without him? I think he did.

I know how bizarre these messages may sound. This is why, when I tell people these stories, I always begin with, "I know this is going to sound crazy, but…".

These stories happen all the time.

My second reading wasn't really my reading at all. Anonymously, my husband booked a session with one of the women who facilitated the workshop I attended. Nothing she said resonated with my husband. Instead, I am convinced that Cameron used that time to talk directly to me.

First of all, she very accurately validated that his passing felt like an allergic reaction and a poisoning, all at once. It had been something systemic that had hit fast and spread rapidly. It was something unusual, given his age. She said it was something that had impacted his brain, and later other organs, one by one.

No one knew that level of detail.

This was significant, because we had just gotten our porphyria diagnosis. He pushed multiple times in that reading on the fact this was an accident. It was no one's fault. There was nothing that could have been done. He wanted us to release the guilt we were carrying.

One of the things my husband wanted to know was whether my son was at his memorial. She mentioned he kept saying "Superman", even though she didn't feel like he was really into superheroes. All four of us had worn Superman shirts for his memorial.

Then, he shifted the reading to a place she said she never goes, but he insisted.

Cameron started answering questions I had been asking myself for weeks.

I had been spending all my time reading about the afterlife, near-death experiences, and asking Cameron constantly what it was like where he was. I was searching for my *why*.

Her exact words were, "He wants his mom to have peace of mind."

She went on to talk about his soul contract. It was a concept I was wrestling with and asking him for guidance on. Much to my husband's annoyance, Cameron used this session to deliver it to me.

Before I share this story, I want to stress that this concept is a bit advanced, spiritually. I know many bereaved parents, and others on this same journey, who do not necessarily believe it. That's OK. I don't share this story to convince you or try to change your mind. I simply share it because it is my story. One of my "I know this sounds crazy, but" stories.

The concept of soul planning is that we pre-plan the experiences we will have during our lives here on Earth. I know what you're thinking. *Who in their right mind would choose this?!*

Basically, we make contracts with other souls who agree to play a role for us. It is a divine plan that we help craft. Our goal in doing this is to fully feel and live the things we cannot experience on the other side. These experiences test us, teach us. The struggle, the hardships we face here, allow us to grow our soul over there.

So, think of Earth like a video game, in a way. We come here and play, potentially many times. We have free will while we are here, to do as we like. Things cross our paths, as they are meant to. Our goal in the end changes, but our path there is up to us. When we achieve our goal, we die.

She said he wanted to talk about the other side.

While he was in his coma, he could hear everyone talking around him. He didn't know what was happening in the moment, but he assured us he felt no suffering. He kept trying to tell us, "I'm OK, I'm right here". We just couldn't hear him.

He then talked about his transition out of his body. A special team of angels helped him transition, they helped all kids.

She also said his passing was intended to spiritually awaken us both. It was part of the plan. He assured us that even if he hadn't died that night, something else would have happened shortly after, because his contract was up. He had done what he was meant to do. For this reason, he was at peace.

She then ended by sharing three things that were validating to me:

First, he said he didn't like what they did to his hair. At the hospital, they had shaved some of his hair. We had received it in a bag, along with his hand and footprints.

Second, she referenced the AC going out in my car and it being really hot. The month before, I had driven our old red car to the airport for my first trip out of town. On my way to the airport, the AC went out, and I had sweated the entire car ride to the airport! No one had known about the AC.

Third, he shared that his birth story was funny. I went in for a normal checkup at 38 weeks. He was breech. The doctor had looked at me and said, "We need to schedule you for a c-section. How is tonight at 5?" This was totally unexpected! The funniest part, however, came as she had pulled him out. All I heard was the doctor scream. She then reassured me everything was fine. He had just started peeing all over her. That story wasn't common knowledge.

Over the years, I've had some other medium readings. Each was validating, in its own way.

One medium I saw was completely last minute. I was there with a friend. He had an opening and took me as a walk-in. This is the reading that made my husband begin to open up.

I was asked who drives a BMW. I had no clue, as it didn't fit anywhere for me. He was adamant that it was a BMW convertible, light blue, and it belonged to my dad. I knew my dad to have a Cadillac, but nothing that was blue or a convertible, so I told him no and he moved on.

We were visiting family that week. The next morning, my dad called. He was scheduled to pick up my oldest daughter for the day. He asked if I would be OK if he drove the convertible to get her.

I abruptly stopped him and asked, "What convertible?" He said the BMW. Totally shocked, I inquired what color it was. By that point, he was confused by my level of interest in the detail and responded, "Blue, why?!"

I nearly collapsed on the floor! How could that medium have known this vehicle even existed when I didn't?

There are so many smaller stories I could include, seemingly small, but powerful.

I have found every medium is different in the level of detail they can bring through to the living world. While some readings were so much better than others, each brought its own validation. My advice to you is to always do your own research. Also, don't be afraid to make the appointment! The right medium can change everything!

Chapter 16

There Is A Shift

Last year, I planted a beautiful hydrangea with huge, white flowers. At the end of the summer, literally every single flower and leaf had fallen off. It was a complete shell of its former self. Unrecognizable. I thought it was dead.

I had completely given up on it. Ignored it with plans to rip it out.

Do you know what had happened? Six months later, one of the tiniest little buds began to grow on a barren, broken stick. Only one!

I had just started contemplating how I would replace it, and there it was, a bud, where and when I least expected it could be. So, I dug it up. Transplanted it to a pot on my back patio. I created the best possible environment and gave it lots of love.

The plant came back to life! So slowly... so beautifully. Like witnessing a miracle.

This is exactly what life after loss is like.

You are broken, unrecognizable, ready to die at any moment. Then, something happens, and one day, you notice the tiniest little shift.

I can't tell you how or when, but something inside me shifted. More accurately, it was probably a lot of tiny, seemingly insignificant things that all came together.

As I reflect, these are the things that stand out...

I wrote my grief: raw, honest, and real.

It was incredibly cathartic to sit down and sift through every available word, stringing them together to paint a picture of my pain. Then, I gathered every ounce of courage I had and hit "post" for the world to read. That level of vulnerability is terrifying, but it can also be magic.

I felt seen! I've learned grief like this must be witnessed. We need people to know we are hurting. Other grievers need to know they are not alone.

Just this act of sharing my story, my grief, others have felt seen and understood. It is an incredibly beautiful experience to have others read your words and feel so moved they pour their own hearts out. It is an honor to hold space for them when so many others shrink away and avoid it.

My relationship with my son transformed into something I never could have expected.

Early on, every time I would enter a room that held a photo of Cameron, I would look at it and think, "I miss you SO MUCH!" I imagined my thought being projected in his direction, wherever he was.

Quite honestly, I became a broken record.

I would repeat this phrase over and over. It was the only thought I ever directed at him. Then, I would judge every one of my actions and question if I missed him enough. No amount of missing him was good enough.

A medium reading changed all of that! Cameron told her, "They never talk to me." He also said, "I can feel how much you miss me." He could literally feel what I was feeling.

Those two sentences struck home. So, I changed my behaviors.

I began to focus my attention on finding him. I wanted to be able to see the signs he was leaving and try to strengthen that connection.

I started talking TO my son... still in my head, but exactly the same way I had done when he was here. I would point out the things we would laugh at, highlight places we had gone before, bring his attention to things happening, and solicit his advice. I even invited him to join me when I would go places or do things we would have done together.

I know it may sound crazy, but I realized if I *really* believed he was still there beside me, I needed to act like it. I would often talk about him in the present tense.

These two intentional things changed our relationship. It helped open me up and shift my perspective to see the ways our connection continues. It allowed me to start trusting my own intuition in reading the signs he was sending. Most importantly, I became confident he would continue to show up.

I moved from the belief and hope he was there, to knowing he was there! I can't explain how life changing that was for me. It ignited a spiritual awakening deep inside of me that became a catalyst for my own post-traumatic growth.

While we never want to admit good things can and do follow the death of our child, I became proof. Somehow, this incredibly tragic, bring me to my knees, soul-crushing experience had brought growth. There was now a desire to be the best version of myself, a need to use my pain for something good.

One of the first things I did on this new path was sign up for a grief-related training program. It was a weekend away to focus on learning the tools I needed to better manage my grief. During the first day, I had an ah-hah moment that completely shook me.

I wasn't working on my relationship with my son. I was working on my relationship with my dad.

I was stunned when I realized what was happening. As the facilitator took us through exercises and talked about grief in ways that would give me fresh eyes about the entire grief experience, I was automatically applying everything I was learning to this other relationship.

I was still grieving hard for my son, but this other grief was complicating it and affecting everything. They were intertwined and I struggled.

A light went off for me. Healing was going to take me outside of my grief over my son's death. It would require me to look deep inside myself, analyze my own messed up stuff, and fix it.

I became aware that I was now on a mission to be a better person, to live my life more authentically, and to create a healthier world to live in… and my son was guiding me!

You know what else I discovered? The narratives we use, the stories we tell ourselves and others, they matter!

One of the questions that always follows "How many children do you have?" is "How did he die?" That is, until someone surprised me by saying, "Tell me about your son."

I started rambling on, tripping over my words, totally dumbfounded. It was like an out-of-body experience. I'm not sure the words that came out made sense. My brain was so laser focused on the question because I realized I didn't know how to answer it!

Due to my grief, I couldn't access any of the information I should have used, and I completely drew a blank. I couldn't even tell you what I said in that moment, because I was so distracted; but I do know the story focused more on the tragic nature of his death, not who he was or how he lived.

The guilt coursed through my body!

It was one of those moments you will later replay over and over in your mind. Mad at yourself for not getting it right, also frustrated with your brain for not working properly. Then, feeling shame, because in the present, without the pressure of someone standing in front of me, I *still* didn't know how to answer.

I decided right then and there that I was done not knowing how. So, I wrote a new response.

I dug through my memories and pieced parts of him back together in my mind. I created the story I wanted to tell when someone asked me about him.

I will share it with you now…

Cameron is my first-born, my only son. He made me a mom. Even bigger than that, he changed me in ways I never expected or thought possible. This will sound crazy, but I know I felt the moment he was conceived. I just knew.

When the doctor told us we were having a boy, I remember a feeling of what I first thought was disappointment. Later, I realized it was fear. I had no idea what I would do with a boy! I had a sister growing up. Most of my cousins were girls. This felt so foreign. Yet, those fears quickly subsided.

He turned our world upside down in the best possible way. I never knew how deep my capacity for love was before I had him. He loved with his whole, entire being! He was a complete mama's boy, a rule follower, always concerned for everyone else's wellbeing, always focused on making everyone else feel good.

When his sister would walk into the room with a new outfit or shoes, he would tell her she was beautiful. He often took her by the hand and showed her the ropes of life. Like any sibling relationship, they had their rivalry. When my youngest daughter was born, he wanted her to tuck him into bed, every single night, so he could hold her. He loved both of his sisters fiercely.

At school, he befriended the underdog. He never wanted anyone to feel left out or alone. He was always the peacekeeper. He was a video game addict, talking a mile a minute to explain every aspect of his latest video game obsession. I will always remember the quip he'd use, "Good thing I told ya!" He was wise beyond his years... an old soul trapped in a young boy's body.

He made me brave. He gave me confidence. I looked at life so differently with him in it. I learned so much from him about myself, about life, about love.

My son was 7 years old when he left this world and went on ahead. At that time, child loss was my biggest fear. In those last 12 hours, I couldn't even believe it was our reality. His exit was even more surprising than his entrance. Again, my life turned upside down.

His life *and* his death changed me in profound ways. I see life through a different lens, one tainted with grief and loss. But just as before, my capacity to love expanded. It now crossed into the afterlife, where I have found my relationship with him continues.

He is *still* teaching me. He has opened my eyes in so many ways. And now, he walks beside me, continuing to help me become a better version of myself.

Do you see how that narrative provides such a different story?

Now, when someone asks me about my son, the focus is placed on the most important part of the story: *who* he was and *how* he loved. The positive ripple he made, not how he died.

If you have never read the poem *The Dash*[8], by Linda Ellis and Mac Anderson, it is a must. It details why this shift, for me, was critical. It helped me focus my attention and energy in a healthier direction... on my son's dash.

I read of a man who stood to speak at the funeral of a friend.

He referred to the dates on the tombstone from the beginning... to the end.

He noted that first came the date of birth and spoke of the following date with tears, but he said what mattered most of all was the dash between those years.

For that dash represents all the time they spent alive on earth and now only those who loved them know what that little line is worth.

For it matters not, how much we own, the cars... the house... the cash.

What matters is how we live and love and how we spend our dash.

---

[8] Ellis, Linda, and Anderson, Mac. "The Dash Poem". Reprinted with permission of Inspire Kindness.

So, think about this long and hard; are there things you'd like to change?

For you never know how much time is left that still can be rearranged.

To be less quick to anger and show appreciation more and love the people in our lives like we've never loved before.

If we treat each other with respect and more often wear a smile… remembering that this special dash might only last a little while.

So, when your eulogy is being read, with your life's actions to rehash, would you be proud of the things they say about how you lived your dash?

How do I live *my* dash? For a long time, I let the worst moment of my life, Cameron's death, take control of everything else. My grief was in charge, and I felt powerless to change it.

What I learned was that we cannot control the things that happen, but we can control our response to the things that happen. It doesn't feel that way, early on, but in time, we do have the ability to choose behaviors and actions. The choices we made will determine the quality of the rest of our lives.

In grief groups, you always hear people say, "It never gets better". I am proof that it can. With the right actions, it changes. If you buy into the idea that it will never get better, it never will. Who wants to stay in that space forever?!

Grief is constantly evolving. The shift will happen when we least expect it.

Somewhere, along the way, my grief transformed into love. Only love. The most intense, magnificent, powerful version of love I've ever felt before.

Imagine how you would feel if your child walked through the door right now, alive and well. When I paint that picture in my head, and feel it, the overwhelming emotion that comes flooding out feels the same as the intense way I grieved: sobbing. This time in relief and joy, in shock, disbelief, confusion, and a total loss of control.

Grief *is* love.

Chapter 17

Healing Isn't What You Think

We can find healing, even when we don't think we can, and even when we don't want.

It sneaks up on you. Just like those hydrangeas, with new surroundings designed just for you, and a lot of love, life will return, often when you least expect it.

You may be shaking your head right now, doubting my words. That's OK. I know the idea of healing after such a traumatic loss feels impossible.

Before you give up on the idea entirely, hear me out.

Healing is not what you think it is. I have seen so many people get caught up in a limited definition, and they find themselves stuck in this grief with no way forward. Even just saying, "This will never get better," can keep you chained in that place.

We are so conditioned to think of healing as a destination. That once you get there, it's over.

If you cut your finger, just slap on a band-aid. In a few days, the cut is gone. If you break your leg, just wrap it in a cast for 6 to 8 weeks. The break repairs itself. You may need some physical therapy, but with minor adjustments and care, everything goes back to normal.

In almost every scenario we know, healing has an end; but that's not the case with grief.

In grief, healing becomes a daily practice, an intention to do what is best for you. Developing a keen awareness of what's going on inside your mind and body, it's a choice we make every day to put ourselves first, to find solutions and coping mechanisms that work for us, to rediscover who we are now, and to learn how to show up in life as the best version of us.

Healing becomes centered around rebuilding a life we *can* live again. This involves eliminating stress and added drama that will only serve to push us farther over the edge. Establishing boundaries to protect our energy and our hearts requires an understanding of our grief. Learning how to manage our triggers, name and feel our emotions authentically, and to accept what is.

Healing means we learn to carry our grief in a healthier way.

It doesn't ever end. It only evolves, changes shape, and integrates into who we become.

Grief has left sticky fingerprints on every surface. They never fully wash away. It is always still there, in the space they should physically fill.

It is still there… even when you choose healing… even when you've done all the work and feel you're in a good place… even if you're a grief coach, as I am now, and help show others the way… grief can and always will show up. It just looks a little different over time.

In fact, the entire idea of grief changed for me. Now, grief is simply my expression of love for my son! I would never expect or want that to end. I feel honored to carry it.

You should know, our goal in healing is never to make our grief end. Grief not ending does not mean you must live in misery for the rest of your life. Grief and life can coexist. When it does, there is so much beauty.

I know you are once again shaking your head. How is this possible?

In my early grief, I just knew there was absolutely no way I was going to heal from this. Why would I want to? I needed to feel pain to make sure his death had meaning. It wasn't fair for me to still live, when he no longer did. I couldn't possibly imagine living again. I didn't want to!

Through this journey, I have discovered so many ways I was setting myself up for additional struggle.

I felt most connected to my son in my deepest moments of pain. I had convinced myself that in order to find him, I needed to seek that pain, and stay with it as much as possible. This felt like carrying my grief, which is what everyone said I should do. Yet, I also felt so much guilt when the pain would fade into the background. In the moments I realized were good, I would hate myself. Was my son's life not important enough? How could I possibly forget him?

At that time, the idea of healing carried a "forget" component to it. Me feeling better meant I had to get rid of all the sad, negative stuff, and that meant my grief, which in turn meant my son. It was flawed thinking, and it caused me to push real healing away.

I viewed life after as life without him. I was so focused on him being gone... forever. That idea is a really hard one to wrap your brain around, and it takes you to some pretty low places. It exacerbates your feelings of being alone.

Even my thoughts and stories all highlighted the tragic story of my son's death. At the two-and-a-half-year mark, someone in one of my grief training programs asked me about my son. A totally normal question I had been asked a hundred times before. As the words came out, I had a moment of dissociation. Like I was watching myself from the outside. I heard my words, and they rattled me.

I realized that every time someone asked me about my son, my response centered around the fact he had died, not that he lived. The bigger realization came when I tried to construct a new answer in my head. I couldn't do it. By telling these stories over and over, I had unknowingly strengthened my connection to his death story and weakened my connection to my actual memories.

I'm sure you've heard the saying that where your thoughts go, your energy flows. When all of your energy is poured into the most traumatic moment of your life, that trauma bleeds into everything else.

I had reached the point that I knew I would have to make a change.

To get where I am now, I found myself redefining my entire experience. I realized all the ways I had been taught to grieve, from the language I used, to the things I had come to expect of the grieving process that were wrong and unhelpful. Many of them were even unhealthy.

You have to be willing to unlearn everything you thought you knew about grief and life after loss. You must develop the skill of grieving.

While that process is personal and unique to everyone, there are definitely things I knew I needed to stop. Things I knew I needed to start doing differently.

One of the things I did, early on, was test my triggers. While this isn't something I push other people to just go out and do, I unintentionally began my own form of exposure therapy.

What I really did was torture myself. I would purposefully find the things that heightened my emotional response, dredged up the pain, and I would try to stay in it. The reason? I wanted to make myself hurt more, to a level I thought was sufficient, given that my son had died.

Initially, this was a combination of my "stay connected to the pain, stay connected to my son" and punish yourself because of the guilt. Although, it was as if no amount of pain I had felt was good enough.

This early behavior somewhat backfired on me, though. Over time, it was as if my body became desensitized. Really, I think it just forced me to process things subconsciously.

When I learned these triggers were highlighting the things inside of me that I needed to heal, I suddenly had something I could fix. Fixing them didn't make me forget, which poked holes in my belief that healing meant leaving all of this in the past.

I began to push my boundaries and build my endurance in dealing with the reactions that came. This ultimately grew my confidence. I knew no matter what I came up against, no matter how much it sucked, I would be OK; and I was.

I had already survived the worst day of my life. Anything else it threw at me paled in comparison.

Ultimately, the triggers began to lose their power over me. I realized this during one of our trips back to the children's hospital for my daughter's appointment.

The parking garage we use towers above the ambulance bay where we had been transported in that morning, where I was first alerted to dramatic changes in his condition.

Every trip we had made in the past, I parked on that same side of the garage, but I never had the courage to look over the railing. This time, four years later, I felt drawn there.

Why?

I can't tell you, exactly, except that sometimes I just want to reconnect to those moments. This journey places space between where we were and where we are now.

While it used to be torture, it had turned into something else: a bridge between my past and my present, a reminder of a significant moment.

Sometimes it's nice to bridge that space and just remember.

As I peered over the concrete edge that day, my heart fluttered and started racing. My palms were sweaty. I could feel the heaviness of those words, "Things have changed."

I paused for a minute and took it in. I allowed it. Then, I stepped back.

In the pain of grief, there will always be connection with my son. However, I now know that connection also exists on the other side of the pain. I would even dare to say I feel more connected to my son now.

Not everyone likes to hear this part, but there is choice in this.

Healing means making a choice every day, sometimes multiple times a day, about how and where you engage, about learning what you need in each moment and choosing it. Sometimes, you take a step back and protect yourself. Sometimes, you take yourself back to the places that trigger it all.

Like that day at the hospital, I still chose it, for a moment.

It is OK to do so. Even after you have reached a state of "being healed". You will still have moments when you choose the pain. That's a normal part of the healing process. Just be intentional about it.

Know why you are choosing it. Do it only for a moment. Then, step back from it and choose differently. It's a skill you learn in the grieving process. Knowing when to lean in and when to pull back, how to acknowledge all of your feelings and honor them.

In learning to do this, you will become aware of the fact that nothing in this post-loss life happens singularly. It all comes at you at the exact same time. Even competing feelings you never would have paired together before, now make sense... which is why there is so much power in the word *AND*.

My biggest surprise? I could be *both* grieving *and* healing at the exact same time. Just as I could feel *both* happiness *and* sadness at the same time. It was eye opening.

There is no roadmap. There are no stages, even though the world of grief is full of people who reference them. There is no timeline. Time has nothing to do with it. What matters most is what you do with the time, the actions you take.

Everyone reaches their state of readiness at different times and in different ways.

Think of your goal as being one of achieving balance. You will always carry grief. Let it evolve and integrate into who you are becoming. Grief should color your world. How could it not? But it shouldn't become your entire world.

Through this journey, we can take our power back and reach a place where the pain doesn't consume us. A place where grief doesn't constantly steal the show. With practice, it can feel less overwhelming and become easier to manage.

We honor our children by taking their death and letting it fuel our life; for them, with them.

Just as we redefine healing. We redefine living, living *with* grief.

Chapter 18

Living With Grief

This is what we do now. We live *with* grief.

Just as we must learn to grieve, we must learn to live. It can feel counter-intuitive when we don't recognize ourselves and have lost all motivation and interest. It can feel overwhelming. Where do you even begin picking up the pieces when everything feels is so broken?

Living with grief is not like living before. We never go back to being the person we used to be. Life never resumes where it left off. Even when we find happiness again, and we can, it doesn't feel the same.

So, why even try?!

Because your child did not die in vain! Because their life, regardless of how short, had meaning and deserves to be honored. Because you becoming the best damn version of yourself is the way you ensure the positive ripple they started for you, becomes a tidal wave for the world.

Also, because you don't deserve to live the next 10, 20, 30, 40 years in pain. You just don't.

Life after loss is bittersweet. It's not what we planned, what we wanted, or what we would choose. And if I'm honest, it's *HARD*! It takes courage, compassion, and grace. You have to dig deep and be open to the idea that life can be beautiful again, but in a very different way.

Just as grief is a journey, so is healing, and so is living.

Your life didn't end when your child died, though you may have had moments (many of them) you had wished it had. You had merely shifted from living to existing. And of course you did! It makes sense. Every single thing has changed.

That shift made it possible for you to survive. It was necessary. When you're ready, you can shift again.

The shift to living doesn't just happen. You must choose it. It sounds so easy, I know. The reality is that there is a lot of fear in choosing it. Am I ready? What does it mean? Will I forget my child? What will people think? How will it feel? What if I don't know how to make the shift? What if it's too hard? What if it doesn't happen for me? I can't do this.

There is so much fear in living after your child has died. Fear and guilt and self-doubt and uncertainty. It can all hold you back, keeping you feeling stuck.

Believe me, I know how much you just want your old life back. I, too, would give up everything to have Cameron back here with me. Yet, that's just not possible. I've learned the more I fight this new normal, this life without him physically here, the harder it is on me.

I was making it harder on myself! What a revelation.

Early on, I could not have cared less. Everything being hard felt like what the situation warranted and deserved. As time went on, I realized just how unfair and sadistic that really was. This was the hardest thing I'd ever done, and yet I was the one making it harder. I was demanding and yearning for compassion from those around me, and yet I was withholding it from myself.

So, I made the decision to stop.

It sounds so easy. Like all we need to do is just flip a switch, and it all goes away. Unfortunately, that's not how this works. But with that decision, I did set an intention to take better care of myself. To allow the grief when that's what I needed, to allow anything else that finds its way in, and to give myself grace when I fall short of my intention. Believe me, I often fell short.

Compassion and permission are the precise foundation necessary for any healing journey to begin.

But what comes next?

This is what every bereaved parent wants to know. I get it! I wanted to know the exact same thing. I wish I could simply hand you a map, impart miraculous wisdom, or give you an exact checklist, but it just doesn't work like that.

Just as grief is unique to you and your relationship, so is your way forward. Trust me when I tell you that you have everything you need inside you to pursue healing. Also, know that we can be our own worst enemies. Many times, without realizing it. You just need to muster up the courage and the energy to take the reins and forge your own path.

That feels too hard, doesn't it?

I've learned that grievers need hope to help them survive. I did. They get that from other people willing to be transparent about their own journey forward. We sometimes need people to point us in the right direction, model it for us, and help shine a light to help us out of the darkness.

So, I'm going to share mine with you. It's an over-simplified framework based on my own journey with 6 things you can focus on, starting now. My hope is that it will help you gain your own footing to continue. The way you approach each piece will look different than it did for me. That's OK. This is your journey.

#1 Redefine Your Grief Experience

I kept looking for all the ways I could just resume life. I naively thought healing from grief meant returning to the person I was before and returning to my life before... just without my son.

That's not how this works.

We tend to get a lot of pressure, both real and perceived, from the world around us to fit back into the life we lived before. We try so hard, believing our goal is to get "back to normal". The problem is, there is no such thing as normal anymore. The life we lived doesn't exist now. Even if you could get close, it doesn't feel right. Yet, we keep trying.

Why?

Instead, be willing to throw everything out the window, turn life on its side, and find a way that we can re-enter without all of the added burdens. Don't let others' expectations of what this should be, or the ideas you held before you knew this loss, define what this experience is like for you. Make it your own.

Exploring the language you use is a great place to start. What does it mean to grieve? What does it mean to carry this grief forward? What does it mean to heal? What does it mean to die?

If you've been paying attention as you've read through this book, you will know that these words no longer hold the same meaning for me, as they once did. What do they mean to *you*, now?

I found the meaning of everything changed for me. Song lyrics, quotes, platitudes, even common everyday phrases we use in polite social conversation changed. So, I aligned their new meanings and the ways I heard them to fit what I needed this grief experience to be for me.

One of my biggest ah-hah moments came from this redefinition. I realized that if I really believed my son was still present in my life, that we would be reunited, then why was I behaving as if he was gone forever? He was actively sending me signs. Proof that he was still here, just in a different way. So, instead of focusing on living without him, I would focus on living *with* him, in a new way.

#2 Lean Into The Pain, Don't Resist

We don't want to feel this way. We are tired of every part of our lives being drenched in grief. We don't have time for this grief wave to come on and take out everything in its wake.

It may seem easier to distract ourselves with TV, dive into work, or shove our emotions into a box and place them on a shelf. These things are only a temporary fix, if that.

It's hard, but resisting the pain, the overwhelming emotions, and the grief only makes them bigger, stronger, and last longer. Then, our negative, judgmental thoughts creep in and bring with them narratives about our life that just don't serve us. None of this changes or improves anything, it only adds a layer of suffering.

In the resistance, we deny our own needs. We reject our authentic selves. We make things worse.

The next time you feel it, lean into it. Allow it. Hit pause on your life and give it permission to take over, even just for a little while. In doing this, you will find that the waves seem to dissipate faster.

Feeling it is your way through it. Arm yourself with the tools, the patience, and the self-love to let it be. As we know too well, everything is temporary, even the deep pain and grief shift.

This brings us to the next one…

#3 Reach Acceptance

Acceptance is not the same as approval. Just because we accept it, doesn't mean we are OK with it. And if you think acceptance is the final stage of grief, it's not! Remember, there are no stages. I now view acceptance as the beginning of our healing journey.

It's that place where you stop fighting your new reality. Where you commit to no longer spending your energy focused on the things that create more suffering. Where you begin to acknowledge this new person staring back at you in the mirror. Where you open yourself up to the idea that there could still be good left in this "after", but it just may look and feel different.

This is the stage where our focus can shift from all the "what ifs" to "what now". It's also where you begin to search for the things that will help.

Everything I came across after my son died was what I call "butterflies and rainbows". Anyone talking about child loss seemed to be on the other side of the grief. Not only was there no pain associated with the grief, but there seemed to be no grief, only recovery.

None of that resonated with me.

It was as if everyone had just trained themselves to use mindfulness to ignore their natural emotional reactions, or spirituality to completely bypass the grief. Neither was healthy. In our culture exists this need for perfection, a push for constant positivity. It's very toxic. I knew these tools had a place in my healing, but I also knew it would not be in the way I had seen it demonstrated.

Life without pain, challenge, or grief isn't realistic. Even before our children died, we experienced hardship. Just as grief is a normal reaction to loss, pain is a normal part of life, one we must accept.

The only way I authentically knew to move forward was to find the place where grief and life coexist. I knew I needed to find balance. I needed to learn how to hold space for the grief, while also seeking joy.

I knew my grief would evolve, but just as my love would never fade, neither could my grief. I will always see that space where he should physically be, and because of that, I will always wish for him to be there. That wish is my grief.

#4 Self-Care Is Critical

I learned that I had no clue what self-care was. To me, self-care had always meant enjoying life's extras. A day at the spa, a manicure, a hot bath, a girl's night out… not that those are bad, but that's not what I'm talking about here. This is not just about rest, relaxation, and fun.

Real self-care means looking inward to discover what you need, prioritizing your own mental health, and protecting your resources. It's about choosing to cut the stress and drama out of your life, learning to say no, creating and upholding boundaries to gain control over the things we will no longer allow or tolerate in our life.

To do this, we must simplify, declutter our places and our mind, release judgement, negative self-talk, and expectations. We must operate from a place of compassion and empathy, pouring every ounce of love we can back into ourselves.

Self-care often feels selfish, but it's not! It's non-negotiable. We are so conditioned to do whatever is necessary to meet social standards, to care for everyone else around us, and to betray our own needs to make others comfortable. All this does is disconnect us more from our own needs and drain our energy.

Energy is a limited resource. I don't have to tell you how exhausting this journey is mentally, emotionally, and physically. You don't have the luxury of wasting even an ounce of energy on things that don't matter anymore. It's not that other people don't matter now, but your wellbeing matters more.

You are your own caregiver. Your survival, your ability to find life again, depends entirely on your ability to care for yourself, to love yourself.

Self-love is at the core of healing. As we discussed earlier, healing is a daily practice. It means learning to reconnect to yourself, to discover who you are now, to get in tune with your own intuition. Once you know what you need, you build trust and self-confidence by following through and meeting those needs.

You are worth it!

I know in my early grief I didn't feel like I was worth it. In those moments, we behave in ways we aren't proud of. I certainly didn't like myself very much in those days. That dislike spilled over into other areas of my life, especially my relationships with other people.

The way I took my power back was by shifting my focus from the external world to my internal world. I had to fix the things I was doing that made living harder on myself. I had to spend time alone and really get to know myself. I had to protect my own headspace because that was the only way I could begin to show up in life the way I now wanted to.

Through this journey to self-love, I also deepened my connection to my son.

#5 Connection To Our Child

Our relationship with our child continues even after their death. This may seem a little far-fetched, depending on your beliefs. Yet, whether you believe they are still here beside us, sending signs, or in our heart, we carry them forward and maintain a relationship with them.

A critical piece of my healing journey includes my relationship with my son.

It started with me simply acknowledging signs. Then, there was the communication through medium visits. It took me a while to realize that if I believed he was still there, I should be talking to him in the same way I did when he was here.

That changed everything for me.

When I wake up in the morning, I greet him. Before I go to bed at night, I tell him I love him. In between those two things, I talk his ear off. It's no longer centered on the "I love you" and "I miss you", as it was in those early days. I ask his advice, point out our inside jokes, and reference our memories.

When I go places, I invite him to join me. He often shows up in unexpected ways, like a random 12 (that isn't so random), a song on the radio, or a heart strategically placed. Regardless, I intentionally create space for him in the present and look for him.

It can feel a little crazy. There will be people around you that don't get it, but that's OK. They don't have to. You aren't doing this for them; you are doing this for you and your child, and anything that makes this journey easier on you is worth doing.

This is how I bring him forward with me and integrate him into this new life.

#6 Talk About Them, Bring Them Forward Too

There is rarely a moment when I don't want to hear my son's name or remember him. He deserves that much! Often, however, I find the circle of people who will bring him up in conversation, or are willing to talk about him, has been getting smaller over time.

Talking about our kids and sharing our stories is a powerful way to heal!

Society seems to want us to stop talking, or at least only talk in amounts they deem are appropriate. It's like they can only handle so much of it before it seems we aren't "moving on" fast enough or we're staying stuck in the past.

Then, we are conditioned to believe being strong means to hide our pain and emotions, which is tied to their death. In reality, it's the exact opposite! Being vulnerable takes way more courage and strength than hiding it way. It's also so much healthier, but there is pressure to conform. It's almost like everything is stacked against us.

There are so many people that want to help you. People currently in your life. People who have experienced the same loss and share their story. People you haven't yet met. The problem is, not everyone or everything is going to align with your healing journey.

One of the greatest things I have learned is that not everyone fits into the same role they held before your child died, and not everyone is equipped to sit with your pain. Grief is uncomfortable, both for us and for everyone around us. That makes it hard for people to stay.

You need a support system – the *right* support system.

You need an outlet where you feel safe to authentically share the positive, happy memories, and the good-ish days, and the pain.

That's why I don't recommend you do this alone.

Connecting with other bereaved parents is a great place to start. There are numerous Facebook groups and organizations dedicated to parents who have lost a child. Seeking a good therapist can help you process through your traumatic memories. You can also work with a grief coach, someone who is trained to meet you exactly where you are today and give you the tools you need to take the next steps forward.

We all have a responsibility to heal ourselves. By choosing a healing journey, we have the power to impact the quality of the rest of our lives. I couldn't imagine spending the next 40+ years of my life grieving in such intense misery. The choices I made have become a beautiful way to honor my son.

My job as a grief coach is not to heal you and make your grief end. That should never be your goal. It wouldn't be realistic. Instead, my job is to help you normalize your experience, validate your feelings, and offer perspectives and tools that will help you cope.

Over time, you will begin to rebuild a life you can actually show up for. One that isn't consumed by debilitating grief, but instead has you properly armed to deal with the triggers and waves of grief when they come. One where you feel connected to your child, living in alignment with who you are now, supported by the right people, and in the right mindset to seek joy.

It is possible. You only have to choose it. Make the decision that you want things to change. If you aren't sure where to start, I would be honored to help point you in the right direction and share the resources I have available.

You can do this. You are no different than me. Just as my son is cheering me on, your child is still there, doing the same for you. You have nothing left to lose, but so much to gain, like finding your child as they are now, in the present.

You no longer have to live without them. You can live *with* them in a different way.

Acknowledgements

A massive thank you to my husband, David. I know it was a big ask when I suggested we share our story (almost immediately after it happened). You didn't hesitate at all. Instead, you've worked behind the scenes to help me continue telling it and use it as a vehicle to help others. Your support has been unwavering, regardless of how dark things were, how hard it was, and how "out there" my beliefs got.

To our daughters, Melia and Sienna, you are loved beyond words. Your brother's absence is loud, but it in no way diminishes your light in our world. You are our why in this new way of life. Your brother may not be here physically, but he loved you fiercely and will always be deeply connected to you. Thank you for helping us remember him and hold space for him in our family.

A special thanks to Jeff Janssen. Without your nudges and encouragement, this book would likely still be in draft form on my computer. I believe the Universe placed you in my path for a reason. First, to inspire me throughout our amazing Soul Peeps groups. Second, to push me to finish writing and publish. I appreciate you!

Many thanks to those I've met on this journey, both friends and clients. Thank you for reading my words, for sharing your stories, and for trusting me with your deepest grief. I continue to learn from you all. It is an honor to know you and to know your children through you. Thank you for walking this path with me.

To our friends and family who stayed and continue to keep Cameron alive in conversation and memory, you will never know how much that means to us. Thank you for your continued support.

A final thanks to my son, Cameron, for breaking me wide open and then guiding me as I put the pieces back together again.

About the Author

Emily Graham is the founder of After Child Loss. As a bereaved parent, author, speaker, and grief coach, she is passionate about shining a light on the reality of grief and helping others navigate life after child loss. When her 7-year-old son died unexpectedly, Christmas 2015, life as she knew it ended and everything changed. It took years for her to find her way forward.

Sharing her story not only brought connection, but it also highlighted the desperate need for more education, support, and authentic conversation about grief and child loss. Emily's story and writing has been featured in The Huffington Post, Still Standing Magazine, Her View From Home, and Compassionate Friends.

Emily's path forward included becoming a Certified Life Coach and Grief Coach. Her training is ongoing in the areas of grief, trauma, mindfulness, purpose, and spirituality. She helps others understand that healing from child loss looks different from what they might expect, and she brings together all the things that helped her find a way forward and learn to live *with* grief.

You can find information about working with Emily at AfterChildLoss.com.

Made in the USA
Monee, IL
16 April 2023